Delish
rozannestevens

Food Photography and Cover Photograph-Ronan Lang

Food Stylist- Sally Dunne

Graphic Design- Eric Greene

ISBN: 978-1-908817-07-5

A CIP catalogue for this book is available from the National Library.

Printed by Clondalkin Group, Clonshaugh, Dublin 17

Published by Delish Publishing in association with Original Writing

Dedication

Dear Mother and Daddy,

This book is dedicated to you.

Thank you,
For raising me to be a lady, but making me believe I can achieve anything a man can, and more
For showing me unconditional love and unwavering support
For teaching me about hard work, dedication and determination
For making sacrifices to give me the best education and start in life
For showing me lifes' great beauty and great sorrow
Most of all, for loving me for me, and teaching me to dream big.

Lots of love, Zannie

Foreword by Pat Kenny

Rozanne Stevens has been a regular presence on *Today with Pat Kenny* for almost five years. I was on holiday when she first appeared as a contributor, so my first contact with her was as a listener. I was intrigued by the voice, the accent, I was charmed by the warmth of the personality, and I was curious as to whether the food could possibly be as good as it sounded. On my return to the microphone, I was delighted to discover that all the broadcast impressions were borne out by the reality. Although she's a native of the Eastern Cape in South Africa, the voice has been tempered a little by ten years in Ireland. And although you can take the girl out of the Cape, you can never entirely take the Cape out of the girl, so her recipes, which are aimed at the Irish audience, are occasionally coloured by the cooking of her native country. Of course South Africa is a melting pot of world cuisine, so the influences on Rozannne's recipes are many and varied. From time to time, she will even share some of her grandmother's best kept culinary secrets, honed to perfection on the family citrus farm in the Gamtoos Valley. And if Rozanne makes everything sound simple and easy-to-do, that's how it is in her kitchen. She makes her instructions clear, concise and accessible, which talent she puts down to the fact that she is the daughter of a school headmistress!.

I've also come to learn about Rozanne's preoccupations, one of which is healthy eating in the broadest sense: not just avoiding things which might harm you, but actively choosing foods that offer health benefits. She will investigate exactly why your greens are good for you, the presence of vital trace elements, vitamins, the anti-oxidants. Or why nuts or fish oils might be important to a balanced diet. Given her expertise in herbal medicine and nutritional therapy, she brings a whole new dimension to planning a menu. A Rozanne meal will not only taste good, it will actually be good for you as well. Personally I'm also delighted that Rozanne has a sweet tooth, so we're allowed occasional treats which are naughty, but nice!

Rozanne is a member of the Slowfood movement, and she is an enthusiast for native Irish produce, frequently visiting organic and artisan producers in her quest for the best. But she is also conscious that we all live busy lives inside and outside the home, and she demonstrates how to produce good food in a timely way. The definition of Slowfood is that it is the opposite of Fast Food, not that it necessarily takes ages to cook, and Rozanne shows how Slowfood can be quick too! And perhaps more important these days, she regularly shows us how good quality food, cooked at home, can be much more cost effective than the trip to the takeaway.

The artisan food industry in Ireland is a rapidly growing phenomenon, and Rozanne was an early champion of these boutique producers. She has travelled the length and breadth of the country exploring the fare on offer and where possible incorporating them into her food. Why use a famous-name foreign cheese when there is a superlative Irish alternative. We've got to know not just the brands but the people behind the brands as well

Although in so many ways she is the personification of the modern woman, Rozanne also cherishes the skills of the generations that have gone before. Many young people today have lost touch with the forgotten arts of baking and jam making. Rozanne is determined to get us all back with the rolling pin and the cake tin. But she marries tradition with innovation. She will give the standard recipe and then, perhaps for the more intrepid cook, offer her own variations, her own discoveries, whether it be an ingredient she found in a Chinese supermarket or a cheese made on the side of a Kerry mountain, or a berry or mushroom which she has foraged from the countryside.

Above all she is utterly unflappable. We've had our dodgy moments over the years, for example when we first tried frying up a storm in our tiny Studio 7, not realising that the fire alarm would go off, or trying to clear the desk of all the kitchen bits and pieces as a Government Minister hovers, or when somebody else is late and Rozanne has to be propelled rapidly into the studio to fill the gap. No problem! And when my weekly political panel used to sample Rozanne's dishes, we've un wittingly offered a juicy beef burger to a vegetarian, as he looked on ashen-faced. Rozanne immediately copped on, and gave him a recipe for a soya substitute, without missing a beat. Along with all her other gifts ,Rozanne is blessed with the gift of calm.

Whether your'e into feasts or frugality, Rozanne Stevens is an inspiration!

Rozanne and Pat Kenny

The Story of *Ish*

Rather than write the usual list of acknowledgements, I thought I would write a little of the story of how I got to this point, of writing a cookbook. This book came about because of people, not just food. I have been very fortunate to have some wonderful people in my life who have helped me to this point. I am only going to mention the real catalyst points in the journey, otherwise we will be here all day!

Since most of you would know my voice from doing the foodie slot on Today With Pat Kenny, we will start there. I had been doing bits and pieces on Rté with various presenters for a few years, being 'recycled' from show to show. I met Marian Richardson, the series producer of the Today show. Marian had been trying to get me to come onto the show as a guest for quite some time, but I dodged it as I felt quite intimidated. So one summer evening, at the Bridgestone Guide Awards, Marian and another producer, Conor Kavanagh, cornered me and convinced me that I should give it a go. With Chardonnay induced bravery, I said yes. Thank you Marian and Conor for giving me the opportunity, minding me and guiding me over the years.

And so began my first summer on the show. Pat Kenny was away on his summer break, so I got to spend the summer with Tom McGuirk. And we had a ball! A whole summer of fun, food and outrageous flirting. Tom was incredibly good to me and really showed me the ropes. When Pat came back, Tom was quite insistent that the show should give me chance.

It was a big adjustment from a relaxed summer of foodie fun to a more serious, cerebral slot with Pat. I thank him for making me a more mature presenter and giving me more gravitas and credibility. But we always have great fun and the show is honestly the highlight of my week. I admire Pat for his intelligence, knowledge and poise. But most of all his compassion and kindness and the genuine interest he takes. He embraces different cuisines, people and way of life with enthusiasm. Pat is a good sport who is game for anything. Until now, he didn't know that I fed him a black pudding made in the casing of a very smelly sheeps' rectum, known as a 'bung'. Sorry Pat.

My good friends and colleagues, the Today With Pat Kenny production team, have also played a huge part in my development. Kay Sheehy, the series producer, and a very smart lady, has always encouraged me to develop my slot from foodie fun into a more weighty, educational and informative piece. Along with Tara Campbell, Geraldine Collins and Valerie Cox, the team have treated me very well and been very supportive. In return, I hope I have fed them well and entertained them with colourful stories of my life.

The Miele Gallery, where I run *Ish Cookery School* from, plays a very big part in my life. I met Pat McGrath, the MD, and Margaret Crerar, the Gallery Manager, three years ago when I helped develop recipes to showcase the Miele appliances. When it came time for me to develop my career, Pat and Margaret offered me the opportunity to use the plush Miele Gallery to run cookery classes from. And every day I walk into the Miele Gallery, I look around at the luxurious surroundings and tell myself what a lucky girl I am. Margaret, my very good friend, thank you for being my rock and keeping me sane. And Pat, thank you for putting up with my crazy ideas (cooking a whole salmon in a dishwasher) and believing in me.

Literature, drama, writing and communication have always been my main passion, not actually food. I really wanted to study journalism when I finished school, but because I had the 'points' I was persuaded to study law. But now, ten years later, I am living my dream as a writer. Thanks to my wonderful editor in the Irish Independent, Helen Hanley, for giving me a weekly column in the Health and Living Supplement. Helen has the patience of a saint and gives me free reign to write about almost anything foodie. Thank you Helen for making my dream of writing a reality. And for giving me a cracking photographer, Ronan Lang, to take photographs for my weekly column. Ronan and I got on so well, I asked him to do the food photography for the book. Which he did in super quick time, thank you Ronan. And thank you for showing off my good side!

And that leads me to my next 'brand alliance'. This time with Total Produce, who you may know as Fyffes. The International Marketing Manager, Vincent Dolan, was sitting in the airport in Brussels, reading my column in the Indo on broccoli (thank you Helen). He pinged me a mail, and since then I have filmed many many cookery video clips for www.topfruit.com . Vincent, a straight talking Dundalk man, has giving me very sound business advice for my own career, and he keeps me up to date with the latest trends. Vincent very generously sponsors the regular charity events that we hold in The Gallery. Thank you Vincent for all your support with the book and of me personally.

And that brings me to another Vincent in my life, Vincent Cleary, the MD of Glenisk. Vincent and I met through Bord Bía and we have become good friends and colleagues. We share a passion for Irish food and organics as a way of life, I really have learned a lot from Vincent. I recently took on the role of brand ambassador for Glenisk. Or as someone put it, I am the face of sour cream! And yes, my picture is on the tubs of Glenisk organic crème fraiche. And proud of it. Vincent and Emma Walls, the Glenisk marketing director, have worked very hard to help me grow and develop my profile.

Many many things have gone wrong in the journey of producing this book (but that is another story). I am very grateful to my team of designers, photographers, stylist and publisher who have pulled this project together. Drinks on me lads.

And to my friends who I have roped into working with me. Jeff Wilson, Barry Joyce and Fiona O'Callaghan in particular. We have worked hard, fallen around the place laughing, eaten all around us, and cooked more food than I care to calculate. We share so much history together and I am blessed to have you as pals. Thank you for putting up with me and being there for me.

And lastly, thank you Catherine Fulvio, my good pal, for naming my book. Catherine, you are a gem.

I hope to give my readers and listeners many years of foodie fun, enthusiasm and a passion for cooking and sharing. Food is about people, diverse cultures, family, friends and creating good memories.

We're here for a good time, not a long time. Make the most of it.
Lots of love

Rozanne

Contents

Thai*ish*

French*ish*

Italian*ish*

Marrakesh*ish*

Chinese*ish*

Mexican*ish*

Greek*ish*

Span*ish*

P(M)S*ish*

Pantry Pals

Please don't rush out and buy everything on this list. Rather, select a few recipes, and gradually add to your pantry week on week. This means that you wont end up with three bottles of the same thing and wasting money. Try and keep a very tight handle on your stocks, think of your kitchen as a shop. You don't want an enormous 'stock holding' and you also need to use older foods first-Fi Fi-first in, first out. Some of these ingredients may seem a little exotic but I have included a list of preferred suppliers who can help you.

Sunflower oil:
Ideal for Asian recipes and high temperature cooking as it doesn't burn. A flavourless oil so can be used to make bake ware non-stick and as a general, all purpose cooking oil.

Extra virgin olive oil:
Oil from the first pressing of the olive fruit, this oil contains too many flavonoids and compounds to cook with as it burns very easily. Use for salad dressings and drizzling over veggies.

Pure olive oil:
From the second or third pressing of the olive fruit, this oil is lighter in colour and contains fewer of the compounds that can burn. Still only use for low temperature cooking, unless you select an oil that is very pale in colour and therefore few delicate elements.

Avocado oil, rapeseed or grapeseed oil:
These oils are full of healthy fats and make a nice change from olive oil. Select one and try it out in a dressing or for low temperature cooking. Store all oils away from heat and light and preferably buy them in dark glass bottles.

Vinegars:
I use balsamic, white wine, red wine, sherry and cider vinegar on a regular basis. Essential for making salad dressing and marinades. They have a fairly long shelf life, but still store away from heat and light. My current favourite vinegar is a mulberry vinegar I got in the Asian market.

Mustards:
I always have Dijon, wholegrain and English mustard. A low calorie, flavour packed condiment to add instant oomph to anything from a dressing to mashed potato. Store in the fridge once opened.

Herbamare:
This is an organic seasoning made of organic dried herbs and a little sea salt. Only available from health shops, I find this indispensable as a seasoning instead of salt.

Black pepper corns:
I adore black pepper and use it liberally. I prefer crushing my own peppercorns with a mortar and pestle or filling a pepper grinder. Des Crinion, a pal of mine, gave me a present of Cambodian peppercorns-fantastic!

Dried herbs and spices:
Essential for cooking tasty food! Buy good quality dried herbs and spices as the taste is far more pungent. Store in very tightly sealed jars and use within 6 months. I buy mine from OCHo and the Asian markets.

Stock cubes and bouillon powder:
Choose additive free and low salt stock cubes or bouillon. Probably the most widely available brands are Kallo and Marigold. I make up half strength stock so that my food doesn't just taste of stock.

Honey:
Good, local honey is a wonderful sweetener and is full of antioxidants.

Agavé syrup:
This sweet syrup is made from the tequila cactus and has a lower GL than honey. Buy only raw, dark amber agavé syrup from health shops, some brands are very refined.

Tinned chopped tomatoes:
An indispensable ingredient, I buy these in bulk. I have no snob value when it comes to the brand. As long as there aren't lumps of the white stem, I'm happy.

Tomato paste:
I recommend buying this in the tub, unless you are going to use the whole tin at once. I'm petrified of open tins hanging out in fridges breeding botulism!

Sundried tomato pesto or basil pesto:
So handy for spooning into stuffed mushrooms, spreading onto quesadillas or dollying up a piece of chicken or fish.

Peppadews:
These are native to South Africa and are a cross between a chilli and a red pepper. Choose from mild or hot peppadews. They come in a glass jar in a sweet pickling liquid.

Sundried or sunblush tomatoes:
Buy these in oil rather than just dried. Sunblush tomatoes are less dried so sweeter and juicier. So they also tend to go off more quickly. Store them in the oil in the fridge.

Soy sauce:
Kikkoman is a good all round brand, or for a gluten free soy sauce, try Thai Gold or tamari.

Quinoa:
This is my number one favourite grain. The seed of a South American herb, quinoa is gluten free and a perfect protein. Now widely available, I cook it at least once a week.

Oat porridge flakes:
Ireland produces great quality oats, I favour organic porridge oats, either Flahavans or Ballybrado.

Rice:
My favourite rice is organic brown Jasmine rice from Thai Gold. Easy to cook, lovely texture and very nutrititious.

Pot barley:
This ancient grain is fantastic as a chewy, substantial base for salads. And you can throw handfuls into almost any stew or soup.

Dried pasta:
I try and buy spelt pasta as much as possible. It's more nutritious, easier to digest and has a firm texture.

Tinned tuna, crab and salmon:
Great for salads, pasta and fishcakes-no snobbery here!

Lentils:
I use red, brown and puy lentils in a variety of salad, soup, moussaka and lentil cottage pie recipes.

Dried or tinned chickpeas, cannelini beans and kidney beans:
I try and have at least half a cup of chickpeas or beans a day. It's very easy if you use them in dips, soups, salads and stews. Tinned beans and chickpeas are fine to use, but I do like cooking mine from scratch.

Tinned coconut milk:
Thai Gold is the best coconut milk-thick and creamy. Essential in Thai cuisine and great in smoothies!

Harissa paste:
This is a spicy chilli paste made from roasted sweet vegetables like peppers and tomatoes. Spiced up with chilli, gralic, caraway, cumin and coriander. A really versatile condiment, use with lamb, chicken, salmon, vegetables or couscous.

Ready to use noodles:
These are pre-cooked, lightly oiled and vacuum packed. Just break up into curries, soups or stir fries. They come in a few varieties-wheat, rice, singapore-and various thicknesses. Always a great hit with kids and you don't have to faff around with cooking noodles.

Vanilla bean paste:
You can either buy the paste or the liquid extract. These are made from the actual vanilla bean, rather than synthesised. This is a handy ingredient to sweeten baking, muesli, porridge and desserts without having to add sugar.

Freezer Treasures

I have a morbid fear of what I call the CSI freezer-these enormous chest freezers filled to the brim, possibly concealing a dead body. Harbouring frost bitten, cryogenic packages that no one can recognise anymore. They should be banned. My parents generation, having been born during the Second World War, are very conscious of waste and saving everything, and many own a chest freezer. But buying loads of 'buy one get one free' offers and saving every leftover, is a false sense of economy. Minced meat especially, once frozen, gets freezer burn and the meat becomes dry and tough. Leftovers become clingfilm embalmed mystery morsels. If you are very organised, you can cook up batches of soups and casseroles and freeze them in proper freezer containers. I personally prefer to freeze useful ingredients that I can take out, defrost in minutes and whip up a quick meal.

Seeds
Nuts
Petis Pois
Raspberries
Breadcrumbs
Bacon lardons
Chorizo Sausage
Duck breasts
Smoked chicken breasts
Prawns
Parma ham
Smoked salmon
Smoked peppered mackerel
Sliced bread
Good vanilla ice cream
Croissants

Fresh Friends

These are fresh products that I keep in the fridge, fruit bowl and vegetable basket on a regular basis. You will see these ingredients repeated throughout the book. I find it easier to use ingredients, not only for one recipe, but for a wide range of dishes. I find this helps reduce the amount of fresh produce we throw out each week. I use fruit like apples, pineapple and mangoes in sweet or savoury recipes to extend their uses.

I buy meat and fish from my butcher and fishmonger on a weekly basis to ensure freshness and that they get cooked and not discarded. I try and grow a few pots of hardy herbs like sage, rosemary, thyme, lemongrass, mint and parsley. This reduces cost and waste tremendously if you're cooking fresh most days. Every week I also buy other seasonal vegetables and fruits and I really enjoy good artisan cheese. I don't eat a lot of bread, so I tend to freeze it and take out a slice or roll as needed.

Dairy Products and Eggs:
Glenisk low fat milk
Glenisk Greek yoghurt
Glenisk crème fraiche
Glenisk fresh cream
Feta cheese
Mature cheddar cheese
Butter
Organic eggs
Fruit and Vegetables:
Lemons, limes and oranges
Fresh berries: strawberries, blueberries and raspberries
Apples
Pineapple
Mango
Cherry tomatoes
Red, brown and spring onions
Carrots
Celery
Washed and ready to use rocket
Washed and ready to use baby leaf spinach
Butternut squash
Sweet potatoes
Broccoli
Courgettes
Red peppers
Portobello mushrooms
Avocados
Fresh ginger
Fresh garlic

glenisk
ORGANIC
glenisk
for an organic Ireland
ORGANIC
CRÈME
FRAICHE
NATURAL
a cookery class with
Rozanne Stevens
glenisk
ORGANIC
crème fraiche

My dad is a citrus farmer in Patensie, in South Africa. I grew up on 'De Koppen', a verdant farm overlooking the Gamtoos Valley. Norman is a very highly regarded farmer, travelling abroad to share the latest in high tech irrigation systems and new varieties. For all his hard work, he was rewarded with fruit of export quality, supplying Outspan for the overeas market.

So it is very poetic that I am working with Top Fruit to promote cooking and enjoying a diet high in fresh fruits and vegetables. I have filmed many many YouTube video clips with Top Fruit showing you how to prepare and cook fabulous recipes. Many of the recipes in this cookbook will have a video clip on www.topfruit.com showing you how to make it. So have a 'cook-a-long' with me in your kitchen!

Also have a look at the very clever QR codes on the Top Fruit SmartPackaging .

QR codes can be read by any Smartphone e.g. an iPhone. These codes are new - but are very easy to use!

1) Download one of the many free QR Code scanners/readers to your Smartphone from the appropriate site or online store (for example, Apple's APP store). You only have to do this once.
2) Activate the application and point the phone camera at the QR code.
3) Press the scan button/icon.

and don't forget to find us on...

facebook

www.facebook.com/topfruit

Steam Cuisine in a Miele Steam Oven

I haven't owned a microwave oven in over ten years since reading that food cooked in a microwave becomes denatured and is bad for you. I wont do any scaremongering here- you can do your own research on the subject. Suffice to say that many of my students have turfed out their microwaves in favour of traditional cooking methods and steaming food after learning the negative effects of microwaved food.

I am very fortunate that Pat McGrath, the MD of Miele Ireland, presented me with a gift of a Miele Steam Oven for some work I did for them. It has honestly been one of the most useful appliances that I've owned. I have the freestanding model, which can sit on a worktop and be plugged in anywhere- some people even keep it in the utility room!

Steaming is an ancient and very healthy method of cooking food as it locks in nutrients. Traditionally bamboo baskets or more recently, stainless steel steamer pots, were used. In a Miele Steam Oven you can cook large quantities of food and several recipes all at once, making it more efficient. The biggest plus for me is the way steam cooking locks in all the flavour and preserves the nutrients. Even without any seasonings, foods taste vibrant and full of flavour.

And there's less washing up! The Miele Steam Oven comes with solid or perforated stainless steel trays depending on what you're cooking. They just need a gentle wash with soapy water. No scrubbing crusty porridge pots or boiled over rice on the hob! Steam is a natural sterilser, so you just need to wipe out the stainless steel interior on the oven and voíla! You're done!

Oats Porridge
I use organic jumbo porridge oats from Flahavans or Ballybrado. I use equal parts of oats to liquid. For one portion, ½ a cup of oats and ½ cup of water in a bowl, uncovered, is perfect. For a family, use a solid tray instead. Steam for 6 minutes for 1 portion or 8 minutes for up to 6 portions in a tray.
Eggs en Cocotte
In a ramekin, crack an egg and steam on a perforated tray or shelf for 3-4 minutes. For something special, place some smoked salmon, cherry tomatoes, sauteéd mushrooms or spinach in the ramekin first. This will take 5-7 minutes to cook.
Boiled Eggs
Place any number of large eggs on a perforated tray. For a fradboiled egg, steam for 8 minutes, medium for 6 minutes and very soft for 3 minutes.
Green Veggies
In my opinion green veggies should only ever be steamed, never boiled! You lose too many vitamins and flavour. I steam asparagus, broccoli, green beans, frozen peas, mangetout, diced courgettes for 3 minutes on a perforated tray. Bright green and crunchy-perfect!
Carrots
I grew up with overcooked carrots and I just can't stand them. Steam chunky carrots for 8 minutes or smaller carrots for even less. If you use a perforated tray, you can cook them in orange juice with a little ginger or cinnamon.
Potatoes
Peel and cube large potatoes into bite size pieces. Place on a perforated tray and steam for 15-17 minutes. Serve with garlic parsley butter or mash for the fluffiest, lightest mas potato.
Baby Potatoes
Halve baby potatoes and steam for 15 minutes on a perforated tray. Serve as is or use to make potato salad.
Salmon
Add any flavourings or seasonings to fillets of salmon and steam on a solid tray for 5 minutes. For very large fillets it may take 2 minutes longer. The fish is perfectly cooked, moist and delicate.
Ham
I adore a glazed ham, especially at Christmas. But the hours of boiling and watching the ham is so tedious. Steam a ham for 25 minutes per 500g on a solid tray in the steam oven. Add cider and your favourite spices to the tray. Trim the fat and bake as normal after. You will never have such a succulent, moist ham.
White basmati rice
In a solid tray, add 1 cup of basmati rice to 1 cup of water. Steam for 15 minutes. Fluff up with a fork. You can add aromatics like lemon grass, chilli, lime and ginger to the tray.
Brown basmati rice
In a solid tray, add 1 cup of rice to 2 cups of water. Steam for 25 minutes. Fluff up with a fork. You can also cook the rice in chicken or vegetable stock for extra flavour.
Reheating food
Dish up a portion of food and place on the welf or a perforated tray. Depending on how big the portion is, it will take anywhere from 5 to 15 minutes to heat up. Steam is very gentle and will refresh the food, so it will be moist and succulant. You wont be able to burn it, so don't be concerned.

Chapter 1

South Africanish

Anyone that's visited South Africa has seen the incredible sculptures made out of wood, wire and salvaged pieces of scrap metal. In this spirit of 're purposing', this recipe calls for the bread to be baked in used tin food cans. Very eco friendly and funky at the same time! Corn is a staple food in South Africa and this is a typical bread we would serve with a 'braai' or BBQ. It's quite pysical kneading the bread, so you may need one lukewarm beer for the bread and one cold one for the chef!

Tin Can Corn Bread

SERVES 12

Ingredients:

- 1kg plain flour
- 2 t instant dry yeast
- 1 T salt
- 1 T sugar
- 300ml room temperature beer
- 1 tin sweetcorn
- 1 T olive oil
- 150g cheddar, grated

Method:

1. Sift flour onto a clean work service and sprinkle the dry yeast, sugar and salt over the flour.
2. Make a well in the centre and pour in the beer and sweetcorn.
3. Mix gently until its all mixed together but still a fairly wet dough, if its a bit dry, add some water.
4. Knead the dough for 10 minutes until smooth and elastic. Shape into a ball and place in a bowl oiled with olive oil. Cover with a tea towel.
5. After about 40 minutes, knock back the dough and divide into balls.
6. Place the dough into well oiled pots and then place the pots on a baking tray.
7. Sprinkle each loaf with grated cheese and bake at 180°C for about 20 minutes until the bread sounds hollow when tapped.

Biltong is a traditional dried, cured meat from South Africa. Premium cuts of beef and game are selected and spiced with pepper, coriander seeds, chilli and secret spices! A real delicacy, available in South African shops like Jabula in Dublin. Great as a snack, and fabulous in this recipe.

Biltong, Strawberry, Avocado and Papaya Salad

SERVES 6

Ingredients:

Dressing:

- 1 clove garlic, crushed
- 1 jalapenó chilli, finely chopped (you can use pickled jalapenó chiilies from a jar)
- ¼ coriander leaves, chopped
- 2 spring onions, finely chopped
- Juice of 2 limes
- ½ cup light olive oil
- Salt and pepper

Salad:

- 150g beef biltong slices
- 3 avocados, sliced
- 2 cups of strawberries, sliced
- 1 papaya, peeled and sliced
- 1 red onion, very finely sliced
- 200g baby salad leaves

Method:

1. Mix all the dressing ingredients together and adjust the flavours according to your taste.
2. On 6 plates or 1 large platter, make a bed of baby salad leaves. Arrange the sliced onion, strawberries, papaya, biltong and avocado on top. Be careful not to mash the avocado or papaya.
3. Drizzle over the dressing and serve immediately.

*Chutney is like ketchup to us in South Africa, we put it on everything and add it to recipes for depth and bite. The most famous brand of chutney is 'Mrs Ball's', with an original, peach and hot version. My brother Tremaine is the chutney addict in our family, so this recipe is for him. I make up huge batches of this chutney before Christmas as a Festive Foodie Gift-del***ish** *with cheeses, cold meats and any sort of leftovers.*

Tremaine's Curried Tomato Chutney

MAKES 6 JARS

Ingredients:

- 2kg ripe tomatoes, peeled and roughly chopped
- 500g onion, diced
- 250ml white wine vinegar
- 300g sugar
- 2 t salt
- 2 t curry powder

Method:

1. Score the tomatoes lightly with a sharp knife. Plunge into boiling water for a minute until the skin peels back, lift out. Allow to cool for a minute then peel off the skin. Roughly chop.
2. Place the tomatoes and diced onions in a heavy based pot and simmer for 20 minutes until softened.
3. Add the sugar, vinegar, salt and curry powder. Slowly bring to the boil, stirring to dissolve the sugar.
4. Reduce down to a simmer and simmer until the chutney has reduced and is thick and syrupy. Stir constantly! Depending on how soft the fruit is, this may take an hour and a half.
5. While the chutney is still hot, bottle it in warm sterilised jars. Put the lid on immediately.

Sterilising Jars and Bottling:

- If collecting used glass jars, make sure the lids fit securely and haven't been bashed or dinged. Any air getting into the preserve will contaminate it.
- Give the bottles and and lids a good wash and rinse well. Try get the labels off. Boiling the bottles in a large pot of water is very effective.
- Preheat an oven to 150°C and dry the clean bottles for 10-15 minutes.
- Using a funnel, pour the hot chutney into the hot bottles. Close with the lid immediately.

Top Tips:

- Use granulated white or brown sugar
- Only use white wine vinegar, malt vinegar is unsuitable
- Simmer in a good heavy based pot, a cheap pot will 'catch' underneath
- Stir constantly, especially in the beginning to dissolve the sugar
- Cook on a medium temperature, low and slow
- Make sure the lids on the bottles are in good nick, dented and they'll let the air in
- Bottle the chutney while still hot and ensure the sterilised bottles are hot too. Put the lid on immediately.
- Label and date the chutney, try a slanted calligraphy pen
- Cut out circles of pretty fabric and secure over the lid with an elastic band or ribbon

The Malay influence is very strong in South African cuisine and has given us a rich culture of vibrant, fragrant national dishes. The beauty of a Malay curry is that it is warm and aromatic rather than fiery hot. I have kept the spice blend the same but added coconut milk for extra depth. Add exta veggies to bump up the health factor. Served with traditional condiments or 'sambals', a Malay curry will become a firm family favourite. And resurrections the next day are even tastier!

Creamy Cape Malay Chicken Curry

SERVES 6

Ingredients:

- Sunflower oil
- 6 chicken thighs
- 1 onion, diced
- 5cm fresh ginger, grated
- 1 chilli, seeded and finely chopped
- 3 cardamom pods, bruised
- 2 cinnamon sticks
- 1 t ground cumin
- 1 t ground coriander
- 1 T garam masala
- ½t turmeric
- 1 sprig curry leaves
- 6 fresh tomatoes, skinned and diced
- 1 tin coconut milk
- 2 courgettes, cubed
- 1 sweet potato, cubed
- ½ cup of petis pois
- ½ cup fresh coriander
- Basmati rice, to serve

Sambals:

- Finely diced red onion and tomato
- Toasted almond flakes
- Sliced banana
- Toasted dessicated coconut
- Peach chutney

Method:

1. Heat a little sunflower oil in a pot and brown the chicken well. Set aside.
2. Heat a little more sunflower oil and gently sauté the onion, chilli, garlic, ginger, cardamom and cinnamon.
3. Add in the dried spices and return the chicken and add the vegetables. Stir well to coat in the spices.
4. Pour in the tomatoes and coconut milk. Bring to the boil then reduce to a simmer for an hour. Add the peas for the last 3 minutes.
5. Serve with basmati rice and sambals and fresh coriander.

Braaing (BBQ'ing) is akin to a sport in South Africa-it's highly competitive and men dominate the field. My dad is the champion braaier in our family-his lamb chops on the braai ended my stint as a vegetarian! Sosatie is the Afrikaans name for a skewered 'shish kebab'. Meat on a stick grilled on an open fire is the most ancient form of cooking. Bring out the caveman in you with these meaty morsels.

Norman's Curried Beef Sosaties

SERVES 8

Ingredients:

- 2 T curry powder
- 125ml Glenisk Greek yoghurt
- 4 T peach chutney, chopped
- 2 cloves garlic, crushed
- 1 T grated fresh ginger
- 4 T brown sugar
- 100ml white wine vinegar
- 50ml red wine
- 50ml sherry
- 1kg sirloin steak, diced into large bite size pieces
- 2 yellow peppers, diced into squares
- 2 bananas, sliced
- 16 bamboo or metal skewers

Method:

1. If using bamboo skewers, soak in cold water for a few hours.
2. In a food processor, blitz the curry powder, yoghurt, chutney, garlic, ginger, sugar, vinegar, wine and sherry. Reserve 2 tablespoons of marinade for basting.
3. Place the steak pieces in a dish and coat well with the marinade.
4. Cover and refrigerate for at least 2 hours.
5. Skewer the marinated steak with the yellow pepper and banana.
6. Grill on a medium hot braai, basting continuously, for 5 minutes a side. Alternatively, roast at 220°C on a wire rack in the oven for 12-15 minutes.

Boerewors is a traditional South African sausage made from beef or lamb and flavoured with special blends of herbs and spices. Only top quality meat is used and there is much rivalry to produce the best boerewors. I like my boerewors quite spicy with loads of coriander and white pepper. Served on a fresh white roll with Mrs Balls chutney or chakalaka, a boerewors roll is pure bliss. This recipe is ridiculously simple, but it rocks! Butternut squash is widely used in South African cooking and roasts beautifully. The caraway seeds give a nod and a wink to our German heritage.

'Boerewors' Sausage and Butternut Squash Bake

SERVES 4-6

Ingredients:

- 8 boerewors
- 600g butternut squash, peeled and cut into wedges
- 3 red onions, peeled and cut into wedges
- 3 T olive oil
- 1 T caraway seeds
- Salt and pepper
- 450ml chicken gravy (shop bought)

Method:

1. Preheat the oven to 220°C.
2. Mix the squash, olive oil, salt and pepper and caraway seeds in a large roasting tin.
3. Add the sausages and roast for 20 minutes until the sausages are browned and the squash is softened and starting to crisp. Turn once during cooking.
4. Stir in the gravy and return to the oven for a few minutes until the gravy starts to bubble.

This is a recipe my best friend Anni gave me fifteen years ago and is hands down my favourite chicken 'potjie'. This is an Afrikaans word for the three legged cast iron pot that is used to slow cook casseroles in hot coals. The potjie is the image of the witches of Macbeth cauldron, just smaller. Cooking 'potjiekos' (food cooked in a potjie) is close to a religion in South Africa. Along with a 'braai' (BBQ), potjiekos is a male domain with closely guarded recipes and techniques. So sorry for you boys, Anni's potjie is the best!

Anni's Chicken *'Potjie'* Casserole

SERVES 6

Ingredients:

- 2 T light olive oil
- 6 chicken thighs
- BBQ spice to taste
- 250g smokey rindless bacon, diced
- 4 medium onions, finely chopped
- 4 T apricot jam
- 1 T Worstershire sauce
- 100ml water
- ½ small butternut squash, cubed
- 12 baby potatoes, whole
- 12 small onions, peeled
- 300g button mushrooms, whole
- 2 courgettes, cut into half moons
- 1 packet dried white onion soup
- 1 packet dried oxtail/beef soup
- 500ml Glenisk cream

Method:

1. Heat the olive oil in a heavy based frying pan. Season the chicken and fry in the olive oil until well browned. Remove and set aside in a clean dish.
2. Fry off the bacon and chopped onions until golden in the same pan.
3. Mix in the apricot jam, Worstershire sauce and water and stir well to scrape any caramelisation off the bottom of the pan.
4. Transfer the onion mixture and chicken to a large casserole dish or 'potjie'. Cover and bring to the boil, then reduce to a simmer for 15 minutes.
5. Add the butternut squash and baby potatoes and simmer for a further 15 minutes.
6. Add the baby onions, mushrooms and courgettes and simmer for 30 minutes.
7. Mix the soup powders with the cream, pour in and simmer for the final 30 minutes.

Chakalaka is a spiced vegetable and bean dish with a rich, tomato sauce. Born in the townships of South Africa, the flavours are reminiscent of an Indian achar. The recipe is thought to have passed from Indian to African miners and from there it has spread nationwide. Traditionally served with mielie pap (a type of polenta), samp (maize) or as a side dish with braais and stews. I love chakalaka as a condiment in a boerewors roll or as a side salad.

Spicy Chakalaka Salad

SERVES 6 AS A SIDE DISH

Ingredients:

- 1 T avocado oil
- 1 large onion, sliced
- 2 red peppers, sliced
- 1 green pepper, sliced
- 1 carrot, grated
- 1 head cauliflower, broken into florets
- 1 T strong curry powder
- 1 T soft brown sugar
- 5 large tomatoes, roughly chopped
- 1 tin cannellini beans, rinsed and drained
- Juice of 1 lemon
- 4 T chopped fresh coriander

Method:

1. Heat the oil in a large frying pan and cook the onion and peppers until soft, around 15 minutes.
2. Steam the cauliflower for 3 minutes until just tender but still retaining a bite. Refresh under cold water and leave in a colander to drain.
3. Add the sugar and curry to the onion and peppers. Stir well to dissolve the sugar.
4. Pour in the tomatoes and simmer on a low heat for 15 minutes until the tomatoes become pulpy and saucy.
5. Mix through the beans, carrots and cauliflower. Taste and season well with lemon juice, salt and pepper.
6. Transfer to a large bowl and allow to cool completely before stirring in the coriander.

Lee Ann is my-sister-in law, and also a fantastic cook. This salad is one of her inventions and has remained a firm favourite of family and friends for years. It goes well with any BBQ dish and it is quite resilient so wont wilt or go soggy. Your guests will be super surprised that they're enjoying broccoli so much! Many people have asked me for this recipe, and finally I'm sharing it. The secret is to get the broccoli florets nice and small, about the size of a peanut.

Lee Ann's Broccoli Salad

Ingredients:

- 3 heads of broccoli
- ½ cup raisins
- ½ cup sunflower seeds
- 6 back rashers, cooked and cut into fine strips

Dressing:

- 200ml Glenisk crème fraiche
- 2 T mayonnaise
- 2 T vinegar
- 2 T sunflower oil
- 1 T caster sugar

Method:

1. Trim the hard stems from the broccoli. Break into florets and chop into small pieces, about the size of a peanut. You may find it easier to use your fingers to break up the florets. This is key as you want small uniform pieces as the broccoli is raw.
2. Add the sunflower seeds, raisins and small strips of cooked bacon.
3. Mix the caster sugar and vinegar until the sugar dissolves. Add the mayonnaise and sunflower oil.
4. Mix the dressing into the salad. The broccoli florets can clump together with dressing so I use 2 forks to toss the salad.

I serve this instead of Christmas pudding throughout the festive season. It's everything you want in a Christmas recipe: boozy, nutty, spicy and decadent. Served with an orange fragranced strawberry compote to juxtapose the dark, sweet stickiness. Imagine the richest, dreamiest, brandy laced sticky toffee pudding and you're on the right track. Prepare to fall in love with this pudding and to loosen a notch on your belt!

Cape Brandy Pudding

SERVES 12

Ingredients:

- 250g pitted dates, roughly chopped
- 250ml water
- 1 t bread soda
- 100g butter, softened
- 200ml castor sugar
- 1 egg
- 250ml flour
- 1 t baking powder
- Pinch of salt
- 100g pecan or walnuts, roughly chopped

Brandy Syrup:

- 200ml sugar
- 100ml water
- 125ml brandy
- 1 t vanilla essence
- 4 T butter
- Whipped cream, to serve

Strawberry Compote:

- 500g strawberries, hulled and halved
- 1 inch piece ginger, peeled and sliced into 3
- Juice and zest of 1 orange
- 2 T caster sugar

Method:

1. Combine the dates and water in a pot, bring to the boil, stirring. Remove from the heat and stir in the bread soda. Allow to stand.
2. Cream together the butter, sugar and egg until pale and fluffy.
3. Sift in the flour, baking powder and salt and mix lightly.
4. Fold in the date mixture and nuts.
5. Bake in a buttered oven dish at 180°C for 45 minutes.
6. Make the syrup by gently melting the ingredients together in a pot, stirring to dissolve the sugar. Pour the syrup over the pudding when it comes out of the oven.
7. To make the compote, place all the ingredients in a pot, bring to the boil, then reduce to a simmer for 3 minutes. Remove the ginger.
8. Serve warm brandy pudding with whipped cream and strawberry compote.

Chapter 2

Irish

When I first moved to Ireland, smoked salmon was such a novelty to me, that I became addicted! I ate little else but smoked salmon on brown soda bread for the first two weeks. It is advised that we eat two servings of oily fish a week to get all the heart healthy and brain boosting benefits of the healthy Omega 3 essential fats. So here is a great family friendly recipe where you can used smoked, fresh or tinned salmon. If you're super organised, make up a large batch and freeze them.

Salmon Fish Cakes

SERVES 4

Ingredients:

- 300g cooked or tinned salmon (approximate measures, a little less is fine)
- 450g potatoes, peeled and cubed
- 30g butter
- 100ml milk
- 4 spring onions, finely chopped
- 2 T Glenisk crème fraiche
- 2 T flat leaf parsley, chopped
- 1 egg, well beaten
- 1 T plain flour
- Salt and pepper
- Lemon wedges, to serve

Crispy Crumb Coating

- Extra flour for shaping
- 2 eggs, well beaten
- 50g bread crumbs
- 30g plain flour
- Sunflower oil, for frying

To serve:

- Green salad

Method:

1. Boil or steam the potatoes for 10 to 15 minutes until just soft. Drain very well to avoid soggy potatoes and overly wet fish cakes.
2. If using tinned fish, allow to drain very well in a sieve.
3. Melt the butter and milk together in a pot and cook the spring onions for 3 minutes. Season well, add the crème fraiche, flour and parsely, and mash with the hot cooked potatoes.
4. Mix through the egg once the potatoes have cooled a little.
5. Lastly, stir through the fish until roughly mixed to ensure a bit of texture.
6. Dust a work surface or chopping board with extra flour and shape the fishcakes. Dip them in the beaten egg then press into the breadcrumbs to form flattish discs about 5cm thick.
7. Chill for 30 minutes to help them keep their shape whilst frying. These can also be frozen once completely chilled. Wrap very well in clingfilm then freeze in a ziplock plastic freezer bag.
8. Heat a little sunflower oil in a pan and cook the fish cakes for 5 minutes on each side. If you have made them too large to heat right through, pop them into the oven until piping hot.
9. Serve with lemon wedges and salad.

Nothing is more Irish than a beef and Guinness casserole, but in the spirit of ***ish*** *I had to change it up a bit. Guinness is very bitter, so to balance that I took a cue from Moroccan cuisine and added dried prunes to the recipe. They break down and add to the rich, darkly delicious sauce. Every tagine needs a bit of spice, so I chose the allspice berry for another layer of warm flavour. You can add more root vegetables like parsnips and turnips for extra veggie power.*

Beef and Guinness Tagine

SERVES 8

Ingredients:

- Sunflower oil, for frying
- 1.5kg stewing beef in cubes
- 4 T plain flour, seasoned well with salt and pepper
- 1 onion, diced
- 2 T butter
- 2 T flour, extra
- 2 t of ground allspice
- 3 large carrots, diced into thick chunks
- 150g button mushrooms, washed and sliced
- 500ml Guinness
- 500ml good quality beef stock
- 1 small tin tomato paste
- 8 prunes, finely chopped
- 1 small bunch fresh thyme or a bouquet garni (can get them as little teabags of dried herbs)
- 2 bay leaves

Method:

1. Coat the beef well in the seasoned flour. Heat a little oil in a non-stick pan and brown the meat in small batches on a high heat, transferring the browned meat to the casserole dish.
2. Pour the Guinness into the pan and allow to bubble up, add the stock, tomato paste and sugar. Stir well and scrape the bottom of the pan. Pour this mixture over the the beef.
3. In the same pan, melt the butter and gently cook the onion. Sprinkle over the 2 tablespoons of flour and the allspice, stir well. Add this to the casserole dish and mix well. Add in the thyme, bay leaves, carrots and prunes.
4. Cook in the oven for 3 hours at 150°C, stirring every half an hour. Add the mushrooms for the last hour.
5. Serve with colcannon and green beans.

*I love folkore, mythology and all tales of the mystical and mysterious. Ireland has such a rich folkloric history that has even travelled across oceans to be adopted by other countries. Halloween is probably the most famous example. Derived from the Irish festival of Samhaín, to mark the end of the harvest year. Jack O'Latern is actually a villianous character from Irish folklore that was so evil that neither heaven nor hell would have him. Doomed to roam the desolate plain in between, with only a hollowed out turnip filled with a candle to light his way. Irish emmigrants brought Halloween to America, and a lack of turnips led to the pumpkin becoming the ghoulish mascot of Halloween. When I come home, my mom has to make these fritters for me to serve with a Sunday leg of lamb. Very easy, and a del***ish*** *way to use up Halloween pumpkins.*

Monica's Pumpkin Fritters

SERVES 4 AS A SIDE DISH

Ingredients:

- 2 cups of cooked, mashed pumpkin
- 4 T plain flour
- 2 t baking powder
- Pinch salt
- 1 egg, whisked
- Sunflower oil, for frying
- 3 T granulated sugar
- 1 t ground cinnamon
- 3 lemons, cut into wedges

Method:

1. Steam the pumpkin until tender. Leave to drain well and cool down. The more moisture that evaporates from the pumpkin, the less flour you will need and the lighter the pumpkin fritters will be. Mash well till lump free.
2. Mix together the mashed pumpkin, egg, flour, salt and baking powder. The mixture will be quite runny. Cover and rest in the fridge for an hour.
3. Heat a little oil in a non-stick frying pan, drop spoonfuls of batter onto the pan. Fry until golden brown on both sides. Drain on kitchen paper.
4. Mix the sugar and cinnamon and sprinkle over the pumpkin fritters.
5. Serve warm with lemon wedges, which bring out the flavour.

Colcannon is a traditional Irish dish of mashed potato and cooked cabbage. Traditionally served around Halloween, charms would be hidden in the colcannon to predict your fortune for the coming year. If you found a rag-you'd be poor, a bean-you'd be rich, a ring-betrothal and a thimble-spinsterhood. I have taken total ***ish*** *licence and used celeriac (the delicious, knobbly root of the celery plant), sweetheart cabbage instead of traditionally used kale, and fried the cabbage in tea!*

Celeriac Colcannon

SERVES 6

Ingredients:

- 1 T butter
- ½ head of sweetheart cabbage, finely chopped
- 2 T strong tea
- Salt and pepper
- 2 T butter
- 2 tubs of Glenisk crème fraiche
- 6 large rooster potatoes, peeled and cubed
- 1 small celeriac, peeled and diced
- Salt and pepper
- ¼ t fresh nutmeg

Method:

1. Steam the potatoes and celeriac for 15 minutes until just tender. Allow to drain for a few minutes in a colander but don't allow to get cool.
2. Melt a tablespoon of butter in a large pan. Add the shredded cabbage and wilt down slightly. Pour in the tea, season well and cook for 6-8 minutes until the cabbage is cooked to your liking.
3. Melt two tablespoons of butter in a large pot. Add the nutmeg, crème fraiche, season and heat until bubbling.
4. Add the steamed potatoes and celeriac to the hot butter and crème fraiche and mash until smooth and lump free.
5. Mix the cooked cabbage through the mash, check for seasoning, and serve piping hot.

*Ireland is very fortunate to have such an abundance of fresh seafood, so important as part of a varied and healthy diet. I love to experiment with new recipes, but I still come back to old favourites like fish chowder. I fell in love with seafood chowder on a wet October weekeend in Doolin when I moved to Ireland many years ago. I use this basic mixture in several different ways-del*ish *over a baked potato!*

Seafood Chowder Pies

MAKES 6 INDIVIDUAL PIES

Ingredients:

- 50g butter
- 2 leeks, sliced lengthways and then into half moons, rinsed
- 2 small carrots, diced
- 1 clove garlic, crushed
- 2 T plain flour
- 2 small potatoes, cut into 1cm pieces
- 250ml milk
- 125ml Glenisk cream
- 450g firm white fish fillets, cut into 2cm pieces
- 150g smoked cod or haddock, cut into 2cm pieces
- 150g raw shelled, deveined prawns
- ¼ cup fresh chives, chopped
- 2 sheets ready rolled shortcrust pastry
- 2 sheets ready rolled puff pastry
- 1 egg, lightly beaten

To serve:
Irish brown soda bread

Method:

1. Melt butter in a large saucepan and cook the leeks, carrots and garlic for 4 minutes.
2. Add the flour and stir well for 1 minute. Mix the cream and milk and gradually pour in, stirring all the time. Add the potatoes, bring to the boil then reduce to a simmer with the lid on for 8 minutes. Stir occasionally.
3. Add the fish and prawns and poach for 2 minutes. Leave to cool.
4. Preheat the oven to 200°C. Grease and flour 6 large ramekins or individual pie dishes.
5. Cut out 12cm rounds from the shortcrust pastry and press into the dishes. Brush the edges with a little eggwash.
6. Mix the chives gently into the chowder and divide the mixture between the pastry cases.
7. Cut 9cm rounds from the puff pastry and cover the chowder pies. Press the edges firmly to seal and brush the tops with the remaining egg. Cut a small slit in the lid of each pie.
8. Bake for about 25 minutes. Stand for 5 minutes before serving with brown soda bread.

My favourite line from A.A Gill when referring to a dish he critiquéd in a restaurant is: 'The mushrooms wouldn't have been wild if you soaked them in ecstacy and gave them sub machine guns.' But trust me, the mushrooms in Ireland are wild. So wild that you have to go on guided foraging expeditions or 'mushroom hunts' with mushroom experts like Bill O'Dea. Foraging for wild mushrooms (and eating the wrong ones by accident) is one of Europes' most dangerous leisure activities-claiming more lives than any other activity, such as hangliding, combined! Some may call that natural selection.

Wild Mushroom and Spinach Lasagne

SERVES 8

Ingredients:

- 1 box lasagne sheets
- 500g baby spinach leaves
- Light olive oil
- 500g selection of wild mushrooms
- 1 onion, finely diced
- 2 cloves garlic, crushed
- 2 sprigs thyme
- 200g mature cheddar or Gruyére cheese, grated
- Salt and pepper
- Fresh nutmeg

Bechamél sauce:

- 60g butter
- 60g plain flour
- 1 litre milk
- Salt and pepper
- Fresh nutmeg

Method:

1. Clean the mushrooms by wiping with a damp cloth and slice. Heat the oil till very hot and fry the mushrooms in batches till golden. Set aside.
2. Heat a little more oil and gently fry the onion, garlic and thyme till softened.
3. Wilt down the spinach by adding a handful at a time to the hot pan and stirring it in. The heat will wilt down the leaves, just be patient.
4. Remove the thyme twigs. Mix with the cooked mushrooms, season with salt, pepper and nutmeg.
5. To make the white sauce, melt the butter in a pot. Stir in the flour and cook out for a minute. Gradually add the milk and whisk to remove any lumps. Boil for 2 minutes. Season with salt, pepper and nutmeg.
6. Grease a lasagne dish. Pour in enough white sauce to cover the bottom of the dish. Place down a pasta layer. Spoon over half the spinach and mushrooms. Repeat, finishing with a layer of pasta.
7. Cover the top layer very well with white sauce. Sprinkle over the cheese.
8. Bake at 200°C for 30 minutes until golden and bubbling.

When I first moved to Ireland I was baffled and slightly horrified by the coleslaw/ham and coleslaw/cheese combo. In South Africa I'd only ever had coleslaw as a salad with a 'braai' (BBQ). Now I secretly enjoy this mayonnaisey concoction on a crusty roll! A real superfood, cabbage is such an integral part of Irish cuisine that I decided to give coleslaw the ***ish*** *makeover. Use red cabbage, add another Irish superfood-seaweed and lots of super seeds and sprouted seeds and you have a super slaw. The dressing in this recipe is a lighter, zingier alternative to plain mayonnaise.*

Superfood Slaw

SERVES 8 AS A SIDE DISH

Ingredients:

- ½ small red cabbage, finely sliced, a mandolin or food processor attachement is the best
- 3 medium carrots, peeled and coursely grated
- 1 apple, sliced
- 6 radishes, thinly sliced
- ½ red onion, finely chopped
- 4 T dried cranberries
- 2 T sunflower seeds
- 2 T pumpkin seeds
- 2 T dulse seaweed or 'seaweed salad' mix from a health shop
- 100g alfalfa sprouts or pea shoots

Dressing:

- ½ tub Glenisk crème fraiche
- 3 T apple cider vinegar
- 1 T sunflower oil
- 2 t agavé syrup or honey

Method:

1. Mix the dressing by dissolving the agavé syrup in the vinegar first. Then whisk in the sunflower oil and crème fraiche. If you like your dressing a little tarter, add more vinegar.
2. Soak the seaweed in boiling water for 20 minutes if required, depending on the variety you're using.
3. Lightly toast the sunflower seeds and pumpkin seeds in a clean dry pan for extra flavour, allow to cool. This is optional but adds a toasty element.
4. Mix together all the prepared vegetables, seaweed, dried fruit and seeds.
5. Add the dressing and mix well.
6. Scatter over the alfalfa shoots for added crunch and colour.

Barley and leeks are an integral part of traditional Irish cuisine. I love sweet and savoury leeks and I've rediscovered barley as a staple Pantry Pal. I've given them the ***ish*** *factor with a really tasty dressing, toasty hazelnuts and roasted butternut squash. This is a very robust salad or side dish that will travel well as a packed lunch for work and will keep fresh in the fridge for three days. Barley is an excellent source of slow release energy and colon cleansing fibre. Pot barley is the unrefined, healthier option whereas pearl barley has been polished, but is still highly nutritious.*

Barley, Butternut, Leek and Hazelnut Salad

SERVES 4

Ingredients:

- 250g pot or pearl barley
- 750ml stock
- ½ butternut squash or piece of pumpkin, peeled and diced
- ¼ t cayenne pepper
- 3 large leeks, trimmed, sliced and washed
- 2 T chopped parsley
- Olive oil

Dressing:

- 5 cm fresh ginger, grated
- 3 garlic cloves, crushed
- 100ml extra virgin olive oil
- 2 T apple cider vinegar
- 2 T soy sauce
- 1 t wholegrain mustard
- 1 t honey
- Salt and pepper

Method:

1. Rinse the barley well and simmer in the stock for an hour and a half until just tender. Add more water if needed if the barley is still not cooked through. Be sure to cook out the water completely so that the wet barley doesn't make for a soggy salad.
2. Lightly coat the butternut squash with olive oil, season with salt, pepper and a sprinkling of cayenne pepper. Spread out on a baking tray and roast for 20 minutes at 200°C until just tender and starting to caramelise.
3. Mix the dressing and pour over the warm cooked barley. Season to taste.
4. Gently cook the leeks in a little olive oil and mix through the barley.
5. Fold in the roasted butternut squash, be careful nor to mush it.
6. Garnish with chopped toasted hazelnuts and parsley.

I never reallly enjoyed porridge until I moved to Ireland, now I love it for breakfast with fruit and yoghurt. The Irish soil and climate produces highly nutritious, good quality oats. The grains fluff up really well and have a lovely texture, not boarding school gloop! This is a great recipe to enjoy even more of this supergrain and very family friendly. Make up the batter and keep it in the fridge for weekend brekkie, just add a little more milk if it gets too thick. Serve with plenty of fresh seasonal fruit and Greek yoghurt. Delish!

Oaty Pancakes

SERVES 6

Ingredients:

- 150g plain flour
- 100g wholemeal flour
- 100g porridge oats
- 2 t baking powder
- pinch salt
- 50g sugar
- 2 eggs
- 2 T sunflower oil, plus extra for frying
- 500ml Glenisk milk
- Fresh fruit, maple syrup and Glenisk Greek yoghurt to serve

Method:

1. Whisk together the oil, milk and eggs.
2. Sift together the flours, salt and baking powder into a bowl. Stir in the oats and mix well.
3. Make a well in the centre of the dry ingredients and pour in the liquid.
4. Mix well then allow to rest in the fridge for 20 minutes.
5. Heat a little sunflower oil in a non-stick pan.
6. Use one tablespoon of batter for each pancake and plop into frying pan. Cook for three minutes on each side. Keep warm while you make the rest of the pancakes.
7. Serve with maple syrup, fruit and yoghurt.

My mom has been making this recipe for as long as I can rememeber. First, you bake the appley, cinnamony sponge, then you pour the steaming, rich caramel sauce over and allow it to sink in. Heaven with cream or custard. There are 140 varieties of apples that are native to Ireland with wonderful names like 'Cavan Rose' and 'Irish Molly'. Any eating or cooking apple will work, so have fun experimenting with different types, not the same old same old!

Monica's Apple Caramel Sponge

Ingredients:

- 4 apples, peeled, cored and diced into bite size pieces
- 1 cup sugar
- 180g butter
- 1 t baking powder
- 2 eggs
- Pinch salt
- 2 cups self-raising flour
- 1 cup milk
- Cinnamon sugar (1 T sugar mixed with 2 t ground cinnamon)

Caramel sauce

- 1 cup sugar
- 250ml Glenisk cream
- 1 t vanilla essence
- 50g butter

Method:

1. Preheat the oven to 180°C. Butter a lasagne type baking dish.
2. Cream together the butter and sugar until pale and fluffy. Beat the eggs in one at a time.
3. Add in the milk graduallly and beat well.
4. Sift in the flour, baking powder and salt and slowly mix in.
5. Pour the batter into the greased baking dish. Chop up the apples and push them into the dough. The sponge will bake and puff up around the apples, so don't push them in too deep.
6. Sprinkle with cinnamon sugar and bake for 30 minutes at 180°C.
7. Simmer the caramel sauce for 15 minutes and as soon as the sponge comes out of the oven, pour over the hot sauce. Be careful not to overcook the sauce as it turns to toffee!
8. Serve with cream,ice cream or custard.

Chapter 3

Thaiish

This is a unusual foodie experiment that I introduce my new students to. At first, people are sceptical and then they really get into it. The idea behind it is to challenge and tickle all your tastebuds so that you are experiencing salty, sweet, sour and heat in different combinations. This helps you to learn how to season food and balance flavours-especially in Thai and Vietnamese cuisine. My favourite combinations are salt and chilli on the pineapple, coconut on the mango and plenty of lime over everything! Good foodie fun with friends to tickle your tastebuds before a meal.

Tropical Tastebud Tingler

SERVES 8

Ingredients:

- 2 pineapples
- 4 mangos

To serve:

- Dried chilli flakes
- Sea salt flakes
- Fresh limes, halved
- Coconut curls or dessicated coconut

Method:

1. Top and tail the pineapple. Slice off the peel following the curve if the fruit. Cut out the black 'eyes' by following the diagonal line in which they run, then place the pineapple on it side and cut slices-they should be a star shape.
2. Peel the mangos and slice off each 'cheek', using the stone as your guide. Slice the mango half into thickish slices and fan out.
3. Arrange the fruit on a platter and set out bowls of seasoning for everyone to make up their own combinations.

This is a very glamorous recipe for entertaining, elegant as a starter. The presentation is special, but not too difficult to achieve. The only challenging element is to make the cashew nut brittle. A top tip is to spread it out on a silicone sheet so that you can get it off! It is very moreish and adds a lovely touch to the recipe. Leftover cashew brittle can be served with after dinner coffee.

Papaya Cashew Nut Brittle Salad

SERVES 6

Ingredients:

- 3 baby papaya
- 1 cucumber
- 2 carrots
- 2 T sesame seeds, lightly toasted
- ½ cup fresh coriander, chopped
- Alfalfa sprouts to garnish

Dressing:

- 5 T sesame seed oil
- 3 T soy sauce
- 1 T rice vinegar

Cashew nut brittle

- 100g cashew nuts
- 250ml sugar
- 100ml water

Method:

1. Mix the sugar and water in a pot, stir well over a medium heat to dissolve the sugar. Bring to the boil and cook until the sugar syrup is a pale golden colour. Pour over the cashew nuts laid out on a silicone sheet. Allow to set then chop up in a food processor or with a sharp knife.
2. Halve the papayas and scoops out the seeds with a teaspoon. Scoop a little of the flesh out into a bowl, leaving the skin and a layer of flesh in tact.
3. Take a vegetable peeler and peel the cucumber into ribbons, discard the watery middle bit. Use the same method for the carrots.
4. Toss together the carrots, cucumber, papaya, sesame seeds, coriander and dressing. Fill the papaya cavities.
5. Garnish with alfalfa sprouts and chopped cashew nut brittle.

This recipe is wonderfully colourful and fresh, perfect as a starter for Christmas dinner. A contemporary alternative to prawn cocktail with marie rose sauce. You don't have to have many presentation skills-the ingredients do it all for you. I get really big juicy frozen prawns from my fishmonger. At a push, you can used cooked prawns, leave out the marinading step and just use the lovely dressing. No need to stress more on Christmas day!

Prawn, Ruby Grapefruit and Lime Salad

SERVES 4 AS A MAIN OR 6 AS A STARTER

Ingredients:

- 20 large tiger prawns, peeled, headed and deveined
- 2 ruby grapefruit, peeled and segmented
- 2 carrots, peeled into ribbons with a vegetable peeler
- 1 cucumber, peeled into ribbons with a vegetable peeler
- 4 T fresh mint, finely chopped
- 1 red onion, very finely sliced
- 100g alfalfa and radish shoots

Marinade:

- Juice of 4 limes
- 1 T sweet chilli sauce
- 1 T kecap manis

Dressing:

- 1 red chilli, very finely chopped
- Juice of 4 limes
- 1 T fish sauce
- 1 T sugar
- 1 t grated lemongrass

Method:

1. Mix the dressing ingredients and leave to infuse.
2. Marinate the prawns for 20 minutes then stir-fry in a wok or grill on a BBQ. They only take a few minutes. They will be done when they are pink, firm and curled.
3. Mix the cucumber, grapefruit, carrot and onion together.
4. Gently toss with the dressing.
5. Add the prawns and work through gently.
6. Serve from one big platter or divide amongst plates.
7. Garnish with fresh mint, alfalfa shoots and serve warm or cold.

This recipe for me is Thailand in a bowl - fresh, fragrant and so good for you. I often make this with prawns instead of chicken. Students are always amazed at how such a simple recipe can be such a taste explosion. The heat level is very mild, so feel free to add more chilli. And for less heat, de-seed the chilli. I use finger length chillies rather that Thai birds' eyes chillies as it's easier to moderate the heat. Extremely figure friendly without any compromise on taste.

Fresh Fragrant Chicken Broth

SERVES 4

Ingredients:

Broth:

- 750ml chicken stock
- 1 stem lemon grass, bruised
- 5cm piece ginger, sliced
- 3 T fish sauce
- Juice of 2 limes
- 1 red finger length chilli, finely sliced
- 150g shiitake mushrooms, sliced
- 1 red pepper, sliced into thin strips
- 3 chicken breasts, sliced
- ½ cup basil leaves
- ½ cup coriander leaves
- 4 spring onions, finely sliced

Garnish:

- 1 red chilli, finely sliced
- 2 limes, cut into wedges
- Fish sauce, to taste

Method:

1. In a large pot, bring the chicken stock, lemongrass, ginger, fish sauce, lime juice and chillies to the boil. Reduce, cover and simmer for 15 minutes.
2. Strain the liquid and discard the aromatics. This is the broth with all the fragrant flavours extracted.
3. Bring the broth back up to the boil and add in the mushrooms, pepper strips and chicken. Cook for 5 minutes until the chicken is cooked through.
4. Remove from the heat and stir through the basil, coriander and spring onions.
5. Serve with fish sauce, lime wedges and extra chilli on the side for your guests to help themselves.

*This is my version of a traditional satay sauce. I use a pinch of chilli flakes for heat in the sauce. As it can be difficult to foretell the heat of dried chillies, I use Tabasco sauce to add a little extra heat at the end if I feel it's needed. Ideally, the sauce should be very gently simmered for an hour to give you a thick, creamy peanutty sauce with nuances of Thai seasonings. As the recipe makes quite a lot, I serve it with lightly steamed tenderstem broccoli-del**ish**!*

Chilli Peanut Chicken Skewers

MAKES 12

Ingredients:

- 4 chicken breasts
- 1 T sesame seeds, toasted

Marinade:

- 150ml soy sauce
- 1 T ginger, grated
- 1 clove garlic, crushed
- 1 T toasted sesame oil
- 1 T sunflower oil

Chilli Peanut Sauce:

- 4-5 T peanut butter, unsweetened
- 400ml can coconut milk
- 2 cloves garlic, crushed
- 2 t grated ginger
- ½ t chilli flakes
- 2-3 t sugar
- 2 t soy sauce

To serve

- Steamed tenderstem broccoli

Method:

1. Soak the bamboo skewers in cold water to prevent charring.
2. Cut the chicken into bite size cubes. Mix the marinade well and pour over the chicken. Leave to marinade for an hour.
3. Thread the chicken onto the skewers.
4. Ideally BBQ, or grill the chicken skewers under a medium grill for 4 minutes each side. Sprinkle over sesame seeds.
5. To make the satay sauce, place the garlic, chilli ginger, sugar and soy in a pot. Gently heat for 2 minutes. Add the peanut butter and mix well. Gradually add the coconut milk, mixing to a smooth paste. Check for seasoning and simmer gently for an hour.
6. Serve the chicken skewers with steamed basmati rice, steamed broccoli and the satay sauce.

I came up with this recipe when I worked as a personal chef. I received half an hours' notice to rustle up something for a business lunch. Eeekk! So this complete makey uppy recipe was born out of necessity. I was complimented very highly on the dish which totally amused me. But this is a very tasty way to enjoy any type of firm white fish and lots of veggies too! Serve with brown basmati or jasmine rice for extra fibre and nutrition.

Easy Red Thai Fish Curry

SERVES 4

Ingredients:

- 2 large or 4 small firm white fish fillets (cod, hake, haddock)
- 1 T red Thai curry paste
- 2 tins coconut milk
- 1 sweet potato, peeled and cubed
- 1 courgette,cubed
- 100g baby corn, halved
- 100g green beans or mangetout, halved
- Juice of 1 lime
- 1 T fish sauce
- 2 T fresh coriander, to garnish

To serve:

- 2 cups brown basmati rice, cooked

Method:

1. Heat up the curry paste with a little coconut milk in a medium sized pot.
2. Add the rest of the coconut milk and all the vegetables except the green beans. Bring to the boil, then reduce to a simmer for 15 minutes, covered.
3. Add the green beans and cook for a further 3 minutes.
4. Lift all the vegetables out of the pot with a slotted spoon. Keep warm in a serving dish.
5. Add the lime juice and fish sauce and stir.
6. Place the fish in the sauce and gently poach for 5 minutes until just cooked. Lift the fish out and serve on top of the vegetables. Pour over the sauce.
7. Garnish with fresh coriander and serve with brown basmati rice.

Duck breast is a wonderfully luxurious meat, perfect for serving on special occasions. Quite often, less costly than fillet steak, duck is my dish of choice for a romantic dinner for two. This dish is more casual though and perfect for entertaining deserving friends. Simplified from the original recipe, it still has plenty of ***ish*** *factor. You'll be tempted to lick the bowl it's so tasty!*

Crispy Duck and Noodle Curry

SERVES 4

Ingredients:

- 2 duck breasts
- 150g rice noodles
- 1x400ml can coconut milk
- 3 T Thai red curry paste
- 250ml chicken stock
- 1 lemongrass stem, bruised
- 1 T brown sugar
- 3 T fish sauce
- Juice of 2 limes
- 150 fine green beans, trimmed and chopped into 5cm pieces
- 100g baby corn, halved
- 1 red chilli, sliced into very thin ribbons
- 4 T fresh coriander, chopped

Method:

1. Prepare the rice noodles according to packet instructions and drain well in a colander.
2. With a sharp knife, slide the blade under the fatty layer of the duck breasts and remove the fat. Slice this into thin strips. Cook the strips in a pan over a medium heat. Let the fat render out and cook until golden and crispy. Remove from the pan and drain on kitchen paper.
3. Slice the duck meat into 1cm thick slices.
4. Pour 2 tablespoons of coconut milk into a pot and stir in the curry paste until fragrant.
5. Add in the rest of the coconut milk, stock, lemongrass, fish sauce, sugar and lime. Simmer on a gentle heat for 5 minutes.
6. Add the thinly sliced duck breast, baby corn and green beans, simmer for 3 minutes.
7. Stir in the cooked rice noodles and heat through for another 3 minutes.
8. Taste and check the balance of flavours. Add fish sauce if you like it salty, more lime for freshness or sugar if it's too hot.
9. Serve in bowls and garnish with crispy duck fat, red chilli and fresh coriander.

These meaty morsels are perfect as nibbles served with drinks. If you can't find chicken or turkey mince, use turkey burger patties or squeeze out the meat from chicken sausage casings, it works perfectly. Kecap manis, used in the sauce, is the thick, sweet, dark, sticky soy sauce from Indonesia. Dark soy sauce will work in a pinch. The meatballs are baked instead of fried to be fat-conscious.

Spicy Meatballs with Sticky Dipping Sauce

SERVES 4

Ingredients:

Meatballs

- 450g chicken or turkey mince
- 2 cloves garlic, crushed
- 1 red chilli, finely chopped
- 4 T fresh coriander, chopped
- 1 egg
- ½ cup breadcrumbs
- Salt and pepper
- 3 spring onions, finely chopped for garnish

Dipping Sauce:

- 2 T kecap manis
- 2 T sweet chilli sauce
- Juice of 1 lime
- 2 cloves garlic, crushed
- 5cm piece of ginger, grated

Method:

1. Preheat the oven to 220°C.
2. Mix together the ingredients for the dipping sauce and gently heat for 5 minutes on the hob. Set aside and allow to cool.
3. With clean hands, mix together the meat, garlic, chilli, coriander, egg, breadcrumbs, salt and pepper. Mould into small meatballs, smaller than golf ball size.
4. Place the meatballs on a lined baking tray and bake for 15 minutes until golden. Do not overcook as they will dry out.
5. Serve garnished with spring onions and small bowls of dipping sauce.

If you're not a big salmon fan, or you are looking to increase your consumption of oily fish, this is the recipe for you! The sauce is delicious-a combination of Thai and French flavours-and transforms the salmon fillets. Served with vibrant steamed green veggies, you can feel very virtuous enjoying this recipe. Asian markets stock banana leaves, fresh or frozen. I often use the frozen ones and leave them overnight in the fridge to defrost. They defrost perfectly and are fabulous used as a tablecloth or to steam fish in little parcels.

Fusion Salmon Parcels

SERVES 4

Ingredients:

Salmon Parcels:

- 4 salmon fillets
- 4 T wholegrain mustard
- 4 T soy sauce
- 1 T honey
- 2 t fish sauce
- Juice of 2 limes
- 2 leeks, sliced and washed
- 2 banana leaves, parchment paper or foil

Steamed Vegetables:

- 1 punnet asparagus tips
- 1 punnet mangetout
- 3 heads of baby pak choy, sliced lengthways

To serve:

- 100g alfalfa/pea shoots
- ½ cup fresh coriander leaves, chopped
- Basmati rice (optional)

Method:

1. Mix the mustard, soy sauce, honey, fish sauce and lime juice together, whisk well.
2. Divide the sauce in 2 and use half the sauce to marinate the salmon in for 20 minutes in the fridge.
3. Wrap each piece of salmon, with a quarter of the leeks, in a banana leaf or make a little foil or parchment paper parcel. Bake the salmon parcels on a baking tray for 15 to 20 minutes at 180°C until just cooked through.
4. In the meantime, steam the vegetables in a steam oven, bamboo steamer or steamer pot for 3 minutes until just tender.
5. Heat up the remaining sauce, ready to drizzle over the vegetables.
6. Divide the steamed vegetables between four plates. Arrange a salmon fillet on top, sprinkle over the fresh coriander and shoots and drizzle over a little sauce
7. May be served with basmati rice if preferred.

A simple recipe, yet quite an unusual combination of flavours. Grilling the pineapple brings out its natural sweetness. While adding a little chilli to the chocolate adds a pleasant warmth. The sour/fresh combination of the minty crème fraiche is the perfect accompaniment to the spicy rich sauce and caramelised pineapple. A favourite BBQ recipe of mine, but one that can be used at any time of year. Great fun for entertaining as it tickles your taste buds but it isn't too far out there.

Grilled Pineapple with Chocolate Chilli Sauce and Minty Crème Fraiche

SERVES 6

Ingredients:

- 1 large pineapple, peeled and cut into long chunks
- Sunflower oil, for grilling

Chocolate Chilli Sauce:

- 1 T butter
- 1 red chilli, finely chopped
- 300g dark 75% cocoa chocolate, broken into pieces
- 250ml Glenisk cream

Minty Crème Fraiche:

- 1 tub Glenisk crème fraiche
- 2 T finely chopped mint

Method:

1. Mix together the crème fraiche and mint, set aside.
2. In a glass bowl over a pot of simmering water, melt the butter. Add the finely chopped chilli and cook for three minutes until soft. Add the dark chocolate to the bowl and melt gently, do not allow the water to start boiling. Once it starts melting, add the cream and heat on a medium heat, stirring regularly. You should end up with a smooth, glossy sauce. Keep warm over a low heat.
3. Coat the pineapple lightly in sunflower oil and grill on a pan or BBQ until golden on all sides.
4. Serve the pineapple with the warm chocolate chilli sauce and minty crème fraiche.

Chapter 4

Frenchish

Mussels are still one of the few delicacies that are reasonably priced. They make a great sharing meal for two or with a group of friends. I have many happy memories of enjoying this French classic with a glass of champagne and good company. Cleaning mussels just requires pulling off the beard, rinsing well and taking off shattered barnacles that can end up in your sauce. While you are cleaning the mussels, if any of them remain open, throw them out. This means that the mollusc is dead and could make you sick. A live mollusc will close when you tap it, as it thinks you are a predator. Conversely, once you have cooked the mussels, any that remain closed should be discarded. So you have two checkpoints to ensure freshness and food safety.

Mussels in White Wine and Fennel

SERVES 6

Ingredients:

- 100g butter
- 2 T olive oil
- 4 saffron strands
- 1 red onion, sliced into thin half moons
- 3 cloves garlic, peeled and chopped
- 2 fennel bulbs, thinly sliced
- 500ml good white wine
- Juice of 1 lemon
- Extra lemon wedges to serve
- 1kg mussels, cleaned and debearded
- 3 ripe tomatoes, diced
- Fresh coriander and parsley to garnish
- Crusty bread to serve

Method:

1. Clean the mussels very well by pulling off the beard and scraping off barnacles. Any open mussels that do not close throw away.
2. In a large saucepan, melt the butter and olive oil and add the saffron.
3. Add the onion and garlic and cook until slightly softened.
4. Add the fennel, white wine, lemon juice and mussels, cover and simmer until the mussels begin to open. Give the pot a good shake. Any closed mussels, discard.
5. Add the tomato, salt and pepper to taste.
6. Garnish with the fresh herbs and serve from the pan with crusty bread.

I'm not a huge pan of pork chops as I think they can be quite dry. But this recipe has converted me. Calvados apple brandy and caramelised apples really transform this dish into a special midweek meal or even to feed friends. Calvados is a great storecupboard ingredient for jazzing up pork and chicken dishes. Equally good in a brandy snifter in front of the fire!

Calvados Pork and Caramelised Apples

SERVES 6

Ingredients:

- 2 T butter
- 1 T olive oil
- 2 red eating apples, cored and cut into 8 wedges
- 4 x 150g boneless pork chops
- 2 shallots, finely chopped
- 100g chestnut mushrooms, sliced
- 1 twig thyme
- 50ml Calvados brandy
- 250ml Glenisk cream or crème fraiche

Method:

1. Melt the butter in the frying pan and gently fry the apples and shallots until golden. Season and set aside.
2. Heat a little olive oil in the pan and cook the mushrooms on a high heat until golden. Set aside.
3. Trim the excess fat from the pork and season well on both sides. Add a tablespoon of oil to the pan and fry for 8-10 minutes. Set aside to be returned to the pan to cook in the sauce.
4. Deglaze the pan with the Calvados and cook for a few seconds.
5. Add the pork chops, cream, mushrooms and thyme twig and simmer for 5 minutes.
6. Season to taste and serve drizzled over the pork with the caramelised apples.

Soup forms an integral part of French cuisine. Not only does soup whet the appetite and wake up the tastebuds for further courses, it has been shown to help aid weightloss when enjoyed as a lunch option. Having soup for lunch aids satiety and curbs calorific afternoon snacking. Science has proven what svelte French women have always known! This is a deceptively creamy, very moreish soup when you need to 'lighten up'.

Creamy Broccoli Soup

SERVES 4

Ingredients:

- 2 T olive oil
- 2 leeks, sliced and washed
- 2 heads of broccoli
- ½ cup cashew nuts
- 650ml vegetable stock
- 250ml rice milk
- Juice of ½ lemon
- Salt and pepper
- Fresh nutmeg

Method:

1. Trim the broccoli stalks and roughly chop. Separate the rest into florets.
2. Gently heat the olive oil in a large pot. Cook the broccoli stalks and leeks for 5 minutes.
3. Add the cashew nuts, stock and rice milk and simmer for a further 10 minutes.
4. Add the broccoli florets and simmer for an additional 8 minutes.
5. Blitz with a handheld blender to a smooth consistency.
6. Season with nutmeg, lemon, salt and pepper.

I adore duck breast, and smoked duck breast is a really special treat. This recipe is perfect for a romantic dinner for two or as a starter for a dinner party. The sweetness of the beetroot and the salty pungency of the goats' cheese complement the smoked duck breast perfectly. Serve with crusty bread to mop up the juices and get tactile. If you can't get fresh beetroot, use the vacuum packed beetroot, but no crinkle cut beetroot in a jar!

Warm Smoked Duck Salad with Baby Beetroot and Redcurrant Dressing

SERVES 4

Ingredients:

- 2 smoked duck breast fillets
- 8 baby beetroot
- 1 pomegranate, halved and seeded
- 100g fine green beans, blanched
- 60g baby salad leaves
- 100g St. Tola's goats' cheese, crumbled
- 2 T walnuts, toasted

Dressing:

- 2 T extra virgin olive oil
- 1 T apple cider vinegar
- 1 t Dijon mustard
- 2 T redcurrant jelly, gently warmed to make it runny
- Salt and pepper

Method:

1. Whisk up the dressing, season with salt and pepper to taste and set aside.
2. If using fresh raw baby beetroot, steam or boil or 20 minutes until just tender. Allow to cool slightly, peel and chop into quarters. Pour the dressing over the beetroot and allow to stand.
3. Halve the pomegranate and break apart to release the seeds. Do this over a bowl to capture the juice. Discard any peel and white pith.
4. Blanch the green beans by plunging into boiling water for 3 minutes. To keep them bright green you can refresh in ice water once they're cooked and drained.
5. Trim any excess fat from the edge of the duck breasts and score a diamond shaped pattern in the fat with a sharp knife. Season with salt and pepper.
6. Place the duck fat side down in a non-stick pan on a medium low heat. Cook for 6-8 minutes to allow the fat to render out and go crispy.
7. Turn over and cook for 30 seconds. Transfer to the oven and cook for 5 minutes at 190°C for medium rare which is the preferred way to serve duck breasts. Allow to rest for 5 minutes then thinly slice.
8. Gently toss the duck, pomegranate seeds and green beans in with the beetroot and dressing.
9. Arrange the salad leaves on the plates, pile the duck and beetroot on top, sprinkle over the toasted walnuts and crumble over the cheese.

The fresh orange juice and zest really lifts and freshens this traditional French classic. And the orange liqueur adds a cheeky punch to intensify the flavour. The long slow cooking ensures tender succulent chicken and a rich, unctuous sauce. Serve with Ginger sweet potato mash and Five Spiced Steamed Greens.

Orange Coq Au Vin

SERVES 6

Ingredients:

- 1 T olive oil
- 1 T butter
- 2 T flour
- 1.5kg chicken pieces
- 6 rashers lean bacon, diced
- 1 onion,diced
- 1 carrot, finely diced
- 2 sticks celery, finely chopped
- 2 T orange liqueur such as Cointreau or Grand Marnier
- 6 T tomato paste
- 2-3 cloves garlic, crushed
- 2 twigs fresh thyme
- 200ml red wine
- 150ml freshly squeezed orange juice
- Zest of 1 orange
- 250ml chicken stock
- 2 bay leaves
- 1 t honey
- 2 bay leaves
- 12 baby onions, peeled
- 200g button mushrooms, wiped clean and halved
- 1 tin haricot beans, rinsed and drained
- 2 T flat-leaf parsely, chopped
- Orange zest, to garnish

Method:

1. Heat the butter and oil in a pan and cook the diced bacon until crispy.
2. Add the onion, carrot and celery and cook until softened.
3. Stir in the garlic and cook for 2 minutes more.
4. Stir in the tomato paste and cook out for a minute.
5. Whisk in the flour to form a paste and pour in the orange liqueur, stir well to get rid off any lumps. Gradually add the wine, orange juice and stock, stirring all the time.
6. Add in the orange zest, bay leaves, honey, chicken thighs and onions.
7. Bring to the boil, reduce the heat and simmer gently for 1 hour and 15 minutes.
8. Add in the mushrooms and beans for the last half an hour.
9. Garnish with chopped parsely.

My dad, Norman, cooks the best steak ever. Normally on the 'braai' or BBQ, but with his top tips you'll get a great result in a heavy based pan. Fillet may be seen as the most sought after cut of steak, but I prefer rib-eye steak any day. It has a great flavour and texture. Also very forgiving of a cook practicing to perfect panfrying steak skills. The creamy mustard sauce is just delish and can be used with chicken or pork instead.

Norman's Sizzling Steak With Creamy Mustard Sauce

SERVES 4

Ingredients:

- 4 X 12 oz rib-eye steaks
- Salt and pepper
- Sunflower oil
- 50ml butter
- 2 small shallots, finely diced
- 250ml white wine
- 250ml Glenisk cream
- 2 T wholegrain mustard

Method:

1. For the sauce, heat a little butter in a frying pan and gently sauté the onion until soft.
2. Pour in the white wine and reduce by half.
3. Add the cream and mustard and simmer on a low heat until thickened. Season to taste.
4. Heat a griddle pan to cook the steaks. Brush the steak with sunflower oil and season well.
5. Cook according to order and allow to rest on a warm plate covered loosely in foil for 3 minutes.
6. Plate up vegetables, arrange the steak on top and drizzle the creamy mustard sauce over.

Norman's Top Tips For Panfrying Steak:

- Take the steak out of the fridge at least an hour before cooking to take off the fridge chill
- Never put salt in any marinade or basting sauce you use
- Coat the steak in sunflower oil, light olive oil or canola/rapeseed oil, don't pour oil into the pan
- Season the steak well with sea salt and freshly ground black pepper
- Heat a non stick pan to high
- Place the steak on the pan, do not move it around
- Allow the steak to caramelise and seal well on that side before turning over with a pair of tongs
- Allow the steak to seal on the second side, if needed, turn once more
- This is as far as you go for a rare steak. For medium rare, turn down the hob a little and cook for a little longer on each side
- Use the finger/thumb pinch test to test for 'doneness'
- For medium or well done steaks, place on a baking tray and finish off in the oven for 8-12 minutes at 180°C until cooked to your liking
- Allow the steak to rest for a few minutes on a warm plate, loosely covered with foil

This is my absolute go to recipe when I am cooking to entertain. Chicken supremes are breasts of chicken with the skin on but the breast bone removed, the ideal cut for this recipe. Serve with Ginger Sweet Potato Mash and Five Spiced Steamed Greens for the perfect taste, texture and colour combination.

Creamy Tarragon Chicken

SERVES 4

Ingredients:

- Olive oil
- 4 chicken breasts or chicken supremes
- 4 small shallots, finely chopped
- 1 T cornflour
- 150ml dry white wine
- 200ml chicken stock
- 400ml Glenisk cream or crème fraiche
- 1 T Dijon mustard
- 3 T chopped fresh tarragon
- Salt and pepper

Method:

1. Season the chicken well with salt and pepper. Heat a little oil in a frying pan and brown well on both sides for about 4 minutes a side. Set aside on a clean plate.
2. Gently sauté the shallots in the olive oil until soft.
3. Dissolve the cornflour in the white wine and add to the pan. Bubble up for 2 minutes.
4. Stir in the mustard, chicken stock and cream.
5. Return the chicken to the pan and simmer for 15 minutes.
6. Stir through the tarragon, simmer for 3 minutes and adjust seasoning.

Crunchy green beans are my favourite classy side vegetable. I serve them with everything from steak, casseroles, lamb shank to roast chicken. If the dish has a rich sauce, I think steamed green beans are the perfect accompaniment. But sometimes it's nice to add a little something extra, a little special touch. These green beans are served with caramelised red onions which have been roasted in the oven. Very little work for maximum results.

Green Beans and Roasted Red Onions

SERVES 4

Ingredients:

- 6 red onions, peeled and cut into 6-8 wedges
- 100ml olive oil
- 200ml balsamic vinegar
- 1 clove of garlic, peeled
- 3 sprigs of thyme
- Salt and pepper
- 400g green beans, topped and tailed

Method:

1. Mix the onions, olive oil and balsamic vinegar in a baking dish or tray. Season with salt and pepper and tuck in the thyme.
2. Roast for 15 to 25 minutes until caramelised.
3. Blanch or steam the green beans for 3 minutes until just tender.
4. Serve the green beans topped with the roasted onions and pan juices from the roasting dish.

This is my version of my sister-in-law, Lee-Ann's famous potato bake. Not remotely a figure friendly option, but the most delicious spuds you'll ever taste! I always make these for BBQ's or else my neighbour, Paul, would be devastated with disappointment. Even better at 1am when the BBQ guests get their second wind! Or to help fortify you the morning after when you have to do the post party clean up.

Lee-Ann's French Onion Potato Bake

SERVES 10

Ingredients:

- 2kg baby potatoes, washed and halved
- 6 brown onions, sliced
- 3 sprigs of fresh thyme
- 250g butter
- 50g dark brown sugar
- 2 chicken stock pots, not dissolved in water
- 500ml Glenisk cream
- Salt and pepper

Method:

1. Steam the potatoes for 15 minutes until just tender.
2. Melt the butter in a large pot. Add the onions and thyme and cook on a low temperature until very soft. It helps to place a circle of parchment paper directly on top of the onions. Be patient as this takes about 30 minutes. Stir occasionally.
3. Stir in the sugar, cream, stock pots, salt and pepper.
4. Preheat an oven to 200°C. Place the potatoes in a roasting tin and mix through the sauce.
5. Bake for 30 minutes until golden and caramelized, remove the thyme twigs.

This is my mom's recipe and it is the easiest, most decadent chocolate pudding. It is like a giant chocolate fondant baked in a lasagne type dish. There are two parts to the recipe, a sponge batter and a sauce. These get made separately and then poured into the dish. They curdle and look strange! However, during baking they separate, and you get chocolate sponge on the top and a rich, dark chocolate sauce underneath. Serve warm with cream or ice cream and fresh or frozen berries.

Some of the solid ingredients are measured by volume in millilitres, so use your measuring spoons for small amounts and your measuring jug for larger quantitites.

Monica's Magic Molten Chocolate Pudding

SERVES 8

Ingredients:

- Sponge Batter
- 60g butter
- 190ml sugar
- 1 t vanilla essence
- 1 egg
- 190ml milk
- 250ml flour
- 1 T baking powder
- ½ t salt
- 2 T cocoa powder
- Sauce:
- 375ml water
- 375ml brown sugar
- 3 T cocoa powder

To serve

- Vanilla ice cream and raspberries

Method:

1. Cream the butter and sugar together till light and fluffy. Beat in the eggs and vanilla extract.
2. Sift together the flour,salt, baking powder and cocoa powder. Gradually beat into the creamed butter and sugar, alternating with the milk until all mixed in.
3. Pour the batter into a greased oven dish.
4. Combine all the sauce ingredients in a pot, stir over a low heat until dissolved then bring to the boil.
5. Gently pour the hot sauce over the batter. It will separate and curdle, but this is as it should be.
6. Bake at 200°C for 30 minutes until you have the sponge on top and the sauce underneath. Do not overbake as the sauce will dry up.
7. Serve with vanilla ice cream and raspberries.

Chapter 5

Italian*ish*

This recipe is a real crowd pleaser with kids and adults alike devouring them. The perfect picnic bag and lunch box filler, although it may be gobbled up before lunchtime! I love serving these at brunch with scrambled eggs and relish and a handful of rocket. The recipe makes large muffins so you may want to make sixteen more reasonable size ones or mini muffins. I use 'handkerchief' muffin cases to bake these in.

Picnic Pizza Muffins

MAKES 12 LARGE MUFFINS

Ingredients:

- 300g self-raising flour
- 80ml light olive oil
- 1 egg
- 150g Glenisk low fat natural yoghurt
- 150ml low fat milk
- 1 and a half cups strong grated cheddar cheese
- 1 t dried oregano or mixed Italian herbs
- 8 rindless bacon rashers, diced
- 6 spring onions, finely chopped
- 150g chopped sundried or sunblush tomatoes

Method:

1. Preheat the oven to 200°C. Line a 12 hole muffin tin with paper cases for big muffins or two trays for mini muffins.
2. Cook the bacon until crispy in a non stick frying pan, drain well on kitchen paper.
3. Mix the olive oil, yoghurt, milk, oregano and egg together.
4. Sift in the flour and barely mix.
5. Stir in 1 cup of the cheese, spring onions, tomatoes and bacon. Don't over mix, leave the mixture quite lumpy. Sprinkle the remaining cheese on top of each muffin.
6. Spoon into the paper cases and bake for about 20 minutes until baked through and firm.
7. Allow to stand for 5 minutes before serving warm with butter or cold in lunch boxes.
8. Cool completely and freeze in plastic bags for up to 2 months.

*This is a total cheat, where you buy all your lovely Italian antipasti ingredients and you assemble them to create tasty, more***ish** *nibbles. If you find canapés too fiddly to make, you will enjoy making this rustic finger food. And if you run out, you can encourage guests to make up their own combo's, people like getting involved.*

Mix 'n Match Crostini

SERVES 6 FOR NIBBLES WITH DRINKS

Base: Crispy Crostini:

Take 2 loaves of half baked ciabbata bread, slice carefully with a bread knife into 1.5cm slices, don't go too thick or too thin. Brush with olive oil and bake on a baking tray in the oven for 10-12 minutes at 190°C until light golden. Don't overbake them as you might be popping them back in the oven to melt the cheese.

First layer-spread on a thin layer of one of the following:

Sundried tomato pesto
Basil pesto
Black olive tapenade
Roasted red pepper paté or relish
Recotta cheese

Second layer-add any combination you like of the following

- Salami
- Parma ham
- Sunblush tomatoes
- Olives
- Artichoke hearts in oil
- Roasted red pepper strips in brine or oil
- Grilled aubergines in oil
- Mozzarella cheese, especially buffalo mozzarella
- Goats' cheese
- Fresh basil leaves
- Anchovies
- Parmesan shavings

Presentation:

I like serving these on wooden chopping boards or pieces of slate. Keep in with the rustic theme by using natural materials. And if it is a function where you have to walk around and serve guests, choose a nice light platter! There are lots of bamboo effect and wooden plates and platters to be picked up for next to nothing.

I picked up the original version of this recipe many years ago in a little book called 'Cheap Eats'. It has turned out to be one of my most popular and practical recipes. Most of the ingredients you can keep in the store cupboard to whip this soup up in minutes. Finely chopped onion, celery, carrots, garlic and herbs are regularly used in Italian cooking as a flavour base. This is called a 'soffrito' and is a tasty and nutritious way to flavour soups and casseroles. I always have these veggies in the kitchen for this

Tomatoey Three Bean Soup

SERVES 6 AS A MAIN COURSE

Ingredients:

- 2 T olive oil
- 1 onion, diced
- 2 carrots, diced
- 2 sticks celery, diced
- 2 cloves garlic, crushed
- 1 t dried oregano or mixed Italian herbs
- 1 tin chopped tomatoes
- 3 T tomato paste
- 750ml vegetable stock
- 1 tin chickpeas, rinsed and drained
- 1 tin kidney beans, rinsed and drained
- 1 tin cannellini beans, rinsed and drained
- 4 T fresh parsley, chopped
- 6 T basil pesto, to serve

Method:

1. Heat the oil in a large pot over a low heat. Add the onion, celery, carrot and garlic. Cook over a low heat until soft but not browned. It can help to place a piece of parchment paper, directly down on top of the soffrito to to trap the steam.
2. Add in the tomatoes, tomato paste and stock. Cover and simmer for 10 minutes.
3. Add the beans and chickpeas and simmer for a further 10 minutes.
4. Season and stir through parsley.
5. Dish up a bowl for each person and swirl through a tablespoon of basil pesto.

This is my favourite concoction that I've come up with. A shopping spree in the farmers' market left me with lots of bits and pieces for an antipasti platter that I needed to use up. And I always have a bag of the superfood quinoa in the cupboard so I married the two together. This is a highly nutritious and exceptionally flavoursome dish, ideal for a Meatless Monday. Also great as a packed lunch instead of an soggy sambo.

Colourful Quinoa Casserole

SERVES 6

Ingredients:

- 2 T olive oil
- 1 onion, diced
- 2 carrots, diced
- 2 sticks celery, diced
- 2 cloves garlic, crushed
- 1 t dried oregano or thyme or mixed Italian herbs
- 1 cup quinoa
- 2 cups chicken stock
- 2 T pitted black olives
- 3-4 artichoke hearts in oil or brine, halved
- 10-12 semi-sundried tomatoes
- 2 fresh tomatoes, diced (optional)
- 1 T sundried tomato pesto or paste
- 150g green beans, cut into short lengths (can use frozen peas)
- 2 T chopped fresh parsley (optional)

Method:

1. Heat the olive oil in a non stick frying pan. Gently fry the onions, garlic, carrots, celery and thyme until softened.
2. Add the quinoa, chicken stock, olives, artichokes, tomatoes and paste. Bring to the boil, then reduce to a simmer for 15 to 20 minutes until the quinoa is coming apart and the liquid has mostly evaporated.
3. Add the green beans and cook for a further 5 minutes.
4. Season and stir through the parsley.
5. Keeps well in the fridge for 3 days and is great for a packed lunch, served hot or cold.

Warning: *this recipe is addictive! The sauce is absolutely divine-smokey chicken, sundried tomato pesto and crème fraiche. I often swop sunblush tomatoes for the cherry tomatoes for extra sweetness and depth of flavour. Serve cold as a pasta salad.*

Creamy Smoked Chicken, Broccoli and Tomato Pasta

SERVES 4

Ingredients:

- 300g dried linguine or tagliatelle pasta
- 1 bay leaf
- 2 smoked chicken breasts, thinly sliced (available from the butcher or selected deli's)
- 1 small head of broccoli, broken into florets
- ½ cup halved cherry tomatoes
- 4 T sundried tomato pesto
- 2 tubs 500ml Glenisk crème fraiche
- 2 T pine nuts, toasted
- Parmesan cheese, to serve
- Salt and pepper

Method:

1. Lightly toast the pine nuts over a medium heat in a clean pan without any oil. Watch them as they burn very quickly! Remove from the hot pan and set aside.
2. Bring a large pot of water to a rolling boil, and add a generous pinch of salt and the bay leaf.
3. Add the pasta and cook according to packet instructions until al denté. For the last 3 minutes, add in the broccoli florets to the pot. Drain well and toss with olive oil to prevent the pasta sticking togther.
4. Mix the sundried tomato pesto and crème fraiche in a pot and heat up gently. Season well.
5. Add in the smoked chicken and cherry tomatoes, simmer for 5 minutes until hot through.
6. Toss the pasta with the sauce and garnish with the toasted pine nuts and Parnesan cheese.

I am obsessed with fennel and so are the Italians. They even go as far as to use the 'female' fennel in some recipes and the 'male' in others as they have different flavours. You can tell them apart by their shape: the female is rounded so it has 'hips' and the male is straight up and down. With juicy orange segments and pomegranate jewels, this makes a gorgeous salad for you dining table, especially at Christmas.

Fennel, Orange and Pomegranate Salad

SERVES 6 AS A SIDE DISH

Ingredients:

- 6 bulbs of fennel, reserve leaves
- 1 red onion, finely diced
- 3 sticks celery, finely diced, reserve leaves
- 6 oranges, segmented, reserve the juice
- Seeds of ½ pomegranate
- 3 T fresh mint, finely chopped

Dressing:

- 3 T lemon juice
- Reserved orange juice
- 6 T extra virgin olive oil
- Salt and pepper

Method:

1. Using a mandolin, finely slice just the bulbs. Discard the tough stalks but keep the leaves for garnish,
2. Mix the dressing well. Taste and adjust seasoning, it should be a little tart. Leave the onion to soak in the dressing for 5 minutes to 'pickle' it slighty.
3. Gently toss the onion, celery, orange and fennel together with the dressing.
4. Arrange on a salad platter and scatter over the fresh mint, pomegranate seeds, fennel and celery leaves.

This is my absolute favourite recipe for pleasing large gangs of hungry people. Most people enjoy chicken and everyone loves robust, tomatoey Italian flavours. The recipe multiplies up very well and leftovers are even nicer. I often serve this with Quinoa and Italian Bean Salad.

Chicken Cacciatore

SERVES 4

Ingredients:

- Olive oil
- 4 chicken breasts, cubed and seasoned
- 1 onion, finely diced
- 2 cloves of garlic, crushed
- 150ml white wine
- 250ml chicken stock
- 2 tins of chopped tomatoes
- 1 T tomato paste
- 1 T baby capers
- 2 T pitted olives
- Garnish, large handul of fresh basil leaves or basil pesto
- Grated Parmesan cheese

Method:

1. Heat the olive oil in a non stick pan and brown the chicken in batches. Set aside in a clean bowl.
2. Heat a little more oil and gently soften the onion. Add the garlic and cook for another 2 minutes.
3. Pour in the wine and allow to bubble up for 2 minutes.
4. Add the tinned tomatoes, tomato paste, stock, olives and capers and mix well.
5. Return the chicken to the pot, bring to the boil then reduce, to a simmer for 30 minutes.
6. Garnish with torn basil leaves or pesto and grated Parmesan cheese.

This is another one of my totally 'makey uppy' recipes, but really tasty and a very versatile, healthy side dish. To make the dressing, you can use plain olive oil, or you can use the herby oil drained from the artichoke hearts and sunblush tomatoes. It's normally a sunflower oil but there are dried herbs and garlic added that give it a lovely flavour.

Italian Bean Salad

SERVES 6

Ingredients:

- 1 tin cannellini beans, rinsed and drained
- 250g fine green beans, trimmed
- 150g sundried or sunblush tomatoes, reserve the oil
- 150g artichoke hearts preserved in oil, reserve the oil

Dressing:

- 100ml olive oil, if not using the reserved oil
- 100ml red wine vinegar
- 1 T wholegrain mustard
- 1 t dried oregano
- Salt and pepper

Method:

1. Steam the green beans for 3 minutes and refresh in cold water. Drain well in a colander.
2. Mix up the dressing and taste. You may need to adjust the flavours dpending on the type of oil that you've used.
3. Mix the beans, tomatoes, artichokes and dressing.
4. Keeps fresh for 3 days in the fridge, although the green beans may discolour from the dressing.

The perfect peach is much prized in Italy when the season for succulent white peaches is very short but thoroughly enjoyed. Baking the peaches in sticky sweet Amaretto liqueur caramelises and concentrates their flavour. Pinkly dribbling frozen raspberries add a naturally sweet flavour without the need for too much sugar. My favourite dessert topping, toasted hazelnuts, are just sublime with this dish.

Amaretto Baked Peaches and Raspberries

SERVES 4

Ingredients:

- 4 ripe peaches, halved and stoned
- 50g butter
- 200ml dessert wine or Amaretto liqueur
- 1 vanilla pod, seeded and keep pod
- 50g light muscovado sugar
- 200g frozen raspberries (do not defrost)

To serve:

- 100g toasted hazelnuts, roughly crushed
- Vanilla ice cream garnished with orange zest

Method:

1. Preheat the oven to 220°C.
2. Melt together the butter, Amaretto and vanilla pod together.
3. Halve and destone the peaches. Place cut side up in a snug fitting round baking dish.
4. Pour over the vanilla syrup and vanilla pod.
5. Bake for 20 minutes until the peaches soften, spoon over the syrup at intervals.
6. Add the frozen raspberries for a further 3 minutes.
7. Sprinkle over toasted hazelnuts and serve with vanilla ice cream and orange zest.

If tiramisu is a 'pick me up' then this is a 'pick me up and put me on cloud 9'. Even the smell of the crushed amaretti biscuits mixed with melted butter will drive your senses wild. A truly decadent and delightful dessert. Serve a small slice drizzled with chocolate sauce for each drooling guest. The fresh berries on the side are essential to balance the richness of the cheesecake filling, and they look pretty!

Tiramisu Cheesecake

SERVES 8

Ingredients:

Biscuit Base:

- 250g Amaretti biscuits, crushed
- 80g melted butter

Tiramisu filling:

- 225g full-fat cream cheese
- 225g marscapone cheese
- 200g sugar
- 1 T coffee liqueur
- 2 T marsala liqueur
- 2 eggs, beaten
- 4 T plain flour

Chocolate sauce:

- 200g dark chocolate
- 150ml Glenisk cream

To serve:

- Fresh raspberries, bluebberies, Chinese lanterns

Method:

1. Mix the biscuit crumbs and melted butter together. Cover the base and sides of a 20cm spring form cake tin with the mixture and refrigerate for 30 minutes.
2. Mix the coffee liqueur, masala and caster sugar together to dissolve the sugar.
3. Add this to the cream cheese and marscapone and beat until smooth.
4. Add the eggs and flour and fold in gently. Do not over mix.
5. Pour into the cake tin and bake for 40 to 45 minutes at 175°C until just firm. If it is browning too much on top, cover with foil.
6. Switch off the oven and allow the cake to cool in the oven.
7. Refrigerate for 3 hours.
8. To make the chocolate sauce, place a glass or metal bowl over a pan of simmering water. Heat up the cream in the bowl until just beginning to steam. Break in the chocolate and stir until melted and glossy.
9. Serve the cheesecake drizzled with melted chocolate and serve with plenty of fresh berries.

Chapter 6

Marrakeshish

Simple, tasty, figure friendly, family favourite, freezes well-this recipe ticks all the boxes. Sweet potato is an economical, highly nutritious root vegetable which is a slow releasing carbohydrate-excellent for energy and as part of a slimming plan. Packed with beta-carotene and vitamin C, sweet potatoes are a vitamin power house. Always a hit with my students, I'm tempted to teach this recipe on every cookery course!

Figure Friendly Sweet Potato and Tomato Soup

SERVES 4

Ingredients:

- 2 T olive oil
- 1 onion, diced
- 4 sweet potatoes, peeled and cubed
- 1 tin chopped tomatoes
- 1litre vegetable stock
- 2 T tomato paste
- 1 t lemon juice
- 1 t ground cinnamon
- 1 tin chickpeas, rinsed and drained

Method:

1. Heat the olive in a large pot and gently fry the onion until soft.
2. Add the cinnamon and sweet potato and stir well to coat the sweet potato.
3. Add the stock, chopped tomatoes and tomato paste. Bring to the boil, then reduce heat and simmer, covered for 20 minutes.
4. Add the lemon juice.
5. Blitz with a handheld blender until smooth. Add the chickpeas. Season to taste.

I'm a bit embarrassed by how easy this recipe is! All that is required is one frying pan with a lid and a kettle. Sauteé some chorizo (or bacon lardons) until the fat renders out, add some gourmet goodies such as sunblush tomatoes, olives, chickpeas and any bits that you like. Pour in a packet of couscous, add boiling water, cover and leave to stand for ten minutes. Bit of crumbled feta cheese, a handful of rocket and voilá, dinner is ready! Change things up according to what you have in the fridge-it is a 'catch all' recipe. Leftovers are great as a packed lunch.

'Catch All' Couscous

SERVES 4

Ingredients:

- 200g chorizo sausage, skinned and diced
- ½ cup sunblush tomatoes or cherry tomatoes
- ½ cup black olives
- 250g tomato flavoured couscous
- 1 tin chickpeas, rinsed and drained
- 100g feta cheese, cubed
- 1 lemon, juice and zest
- 150g rocket
- Olive oil
- 1 lemon

Method:

1. Cook the chorizo in a pan until crispy.
2. Add the tomatoes and olives and heat through.
3. Insert Chickpeas and add the couscous and pour over the correct amount of boiling water. Put the lid on and allow to sit for 10 minutes.
4. Sprinkle over feta and fluff up.
5. Serve up the couscous with rocket on top, dress with lemon juice and olive oil.

This salad makes a very chi chi summer BBQ starter or even main course salad dish. Prawns are so easy to cook on the BBQ, taking only three minutes a side. Sumac is a Middle Eastern spice available in Asian markets and gives a wonderful lemony flavour to the prawns. I only buy my seafood from my fishmonger, as the quality and value is superb. Alternatively, you can find fantastic prawns in the freezer section in most Asian markets.

Sumac Prawn and Watermelon Salad

SERVES 4

Ingredients:

- 12 raw tiger prawns, shelled and deveined
- 1 T olive oil
- 2 t sumac
- 1kg watermelon, peeled and cubed
- ½ small onion, very finely sliced
- 10 pitted black olives, halved
- 150g feta cheese, crumbled
- 150g baby spinach leaves
- 1 T olive oil
- 1 T lemon juice
- 2 T chopped fresh mint

Method:

1. Mix the olive oil and sumac and mix the prawns and marinate for 15 minutes.
2. Griddle the prawns on a griddle pan or BBQ and cook for 3 minutes each side until pink, firm and curled up.
3. Toss together the baby spinach, watermelon, feta, olives and red onion on four plates.
4. Divide the prawns among four plates, drizzle over the lemon, olive and fresh mint.

I've used my favourite super grain, quinoa, instead of the traditionally used bulgur wheat for this tabouleh. Liberal use of orange, lemon and mint make this a very fresh salad, perfect with a spicy meal. Juicy jewelled pomegranate seeds add little bursts of sweetness. And one of my favourite vegetables, fennel, gives crunch and a mild aniseed top note. It's traditional to serve a tabouleh piled into lettuce leaves which makes it a good party dish. A very versatile, visually attractive salad, this will complement almost any spread.

Pomegranate Quinoa Tabouleh

SERVES 4

Ingredients:

- 1 cup quinoa
- 2 cups stock
- 4 T olive oil
- Juice and zest of 1 lemon
- Juice and zest of 1 orange
- 1 cup mint, finely chopped
- 3 spring onions, finely chopped
- Seeds of 1 pomegranate
- 1 fennel bulb, finely sliced
- 150g feta cheese, crumbled
- Baby cos lettuce leaves, to serve

Method:

1. Place the quinoa in a pot with the two cups of stock. Bring to the boil then reduce to a vigorous simmer for 15 minutes until the liquid is gone and the quinoa has unravelled.
2. Fluff up the quinoa with a fork and dress with olive oil, lemon and orange juice, salt and pepper. Adjust the flavours and add more olive oil and lemon juice if you prefer.
3. Mix through the mint, tomatoes, spring onion, pomegranate, feta and fennel. Garnish with citrus zest and extra mint.
4. Serve piled onto lettuce leaves.

I enjoy a wholefood diet using plenty of beans, lentils and chickpeas. I try and have half a cup of one of these a day as they are just so good for you. Besides the health benefits, I love the interesting textures and flavours they add. Avocado is one of my favourite fruits and I would have one on most days. Along with nuts, seeds and oily fish, avocado is packed with beneficial oils. There are many internal benefits I can't see, but I can see the glow in my skin! Perfect as a dip with pita pockets and crudités or as a filling in a wrap.

Avocado Chickpea Hummus

MAKES 1 BOWL

Ingredients:

- 300g dried chickpeas, soaked overnight OR 2 tins of chickpeas, rinsed and drained
- 1 clove garlic, crushed
- 3 t toasted cumin seeds, crushed in a mortar and pestle
- 2 ripe avocados, peeled and chopped
- ½ cup fresh coriander, chopped
- 3 T avocado oil
- Juice of 1 lemon

Method:

1. I prefer cooking my chickpeas from scratch as they have a better texture. Soak them overnight in plenty of cold water. Rinse very well the next day. Add to a large pot and cover with plenty of fresh water. Bring to the boil, reduce to a vigorous simmer and cook for 20 to 30 minutes until just tender.
2. Rinse well under cold water and allow to cool.
3. Lightly toast the cumin seeds in a pan until they begin to pop, do not use any oil. Grind down in a mortar and pestle to a powder.
4. Blitz the chickpeas, avocado, coriander, lemon, avocado oil and garlic together.
5. Taste and season with salt, pepper and more lemon if desired.
6. Serve with pita pockets, crudités or in a wrap.

This recipe is a nod and a wink to Baba Ganoush, the traditional aubergine dip served as part of a meze platter. Incredibly tasty and very moreish you'll become addicted! Served with toasted pita bread or crudités this makes a lovely starter or appetiser. Real sharing food for friends. Also delish served with grilled chicken or lamb as a healthy, fibre packed sauce. It certainly wont go to waste!

Smoky Aubergine Dip

MAKES 1 BOWL

Ingredients:

- 3 large aubergines, halved lengthways
- 2 T olive oil
- 4 t smoked paprika
- 1 whole bulb of garlic
- Juice of 1 lemon
- 1 ½ t toasted cumin seeds, ground down with a mortar and pestle
- Large pinch of chilli flakes (optional)
- 3 T Glenisk crème fraiche (optional)

Method:

1. Preheat the oven to 180°C.
2. Make deep incisions into the aubergine skin. Mix together the olive oil and the paprika and rub into the aubergine, all over the flat side and into the cuts in the skin.
3. Lightly toast the cumin seeds in a small fan until they begin to pop, do not use any oil. Grind in a heavy mortar and pestle to form a powder.
4. Line a baking tray and spread out the aubergines and bulb of garlic on it.
5. Bake for 40 minutes in the moderate oven.
6. Now for the messy bit: scoop out the flesh of the roasted aubergines, discarding the skin. Squeeze out the roasted garlic purée from each clove, discarding the papery skins.
7. Blitz the aubergine, garlic, lemon, and cumin to a rough purée. Taste and decide how the flavours are balanced. Add a little olive oil to thin down the consistency. Throw in a pinch of chilli flakes if you want extra oomph. Or stir in the crème fraiche if the paprika is too hot or you want a creamier dip. I tend to add extra lemon as I love citrus flavours.
8. Serve on a meze platter with toasted pita pockets and crudités.

This is my number one favourite lamb recipe-and that's saying a lot considering my love of lamb! Harissa paste is an essential Pantry Pal-made from roasted sweet vegetables, chilli, garlic, cumin, caraway and coriander. The flavour is warm, spicy and not ferociously hot. Mixed with a little olive oil, salt and pepper, harissa paste will liven up lamb, chicken, salmon, couscous and vegetables. Used here to marinate and baste lamb and vegetable skewers, it caramelises and adds to the smoky charred BBQ effect.

Harissa Lamb Skewers

SERVES 6

Ingredients:

- 4 lamb side loin chops
- 2 courgettes, sliced, skin on
- 1 red onion, sliced into wedges
- 1 sweet potato, cubed/sliced with skin on
- 2 T Harissa paste
- 6 T olive oil
- 1 T balsamic vinegar
- Juice and zest of 1 orange
- Salt and pepper

Method:

1. Place the couscous in a glass bowl. Pour over the boiling stock, stir with a fork. Cover with clingfilm and leave to stand for 20 minutes.
2. Fluff up the couscous well with a fork. Add all the citrus, herbs and olive oil.
3. Season and adjust the flavours.
4. Mix the olive oil and Harissa paste together, season. Coat the lamb and vegetables in the Harissa basting sauce. Skewer onto bamboo or metal skewers and grill on the BBQ. Alternatively, place in a baking dish and grill in the oven.
5. Serve the lamb, vegetables and roasting juices on top of a pile of couscous and a green salad on the side.

I've used my favourite super grain, quinoa, instead of the traditionally used bulgur wheat for this tabouleh. Liberal use of orange, lemon and mint make this a very fresh salad, perfect with a spicy meal. Juicy jewelled pomegranate seeds add little bursts of sweetness. And one of my favourite vegetables, fennel, gives crunch and a mild aniseed top note. It's traditional to serve a tabouleh piled into lettuce leaves which makes it a good party dish. A very versatile, visually attractive salad, this will complement almost any spread.

Pomegranate Quinoa Tabouleh

SERVES 4

Ingredients:

- 1 cup quinoa
- 2 cups stock
- 4 T olive oil
- Juice and zest of 1 lemon
- Juice and zest of 1 orange
- 1 cup mint, finely chopped
- 3 spring onions, finely chopped
- Seeds of 1 pomegranate
- 1 fennel bulb, finely sliced
- 150g feta cheese, crumbled
- Baby cos lettuce leaves, to serve

Method:

1. Place the quinoa in a pot with the two cups of stock. Bring to the boil then reduce to a vigorous simmer for 15 minutes until the liquid is gone and the quinoa has unravelled.
2. Fluff up the quinoa with a fork and dress with olive oil, lemon and orange juice, salt and pepper. Adjust the flavours and add more olive oil and lemon juice if you prefer.
3. Mix through the mint, tomatoes, spring onion, pomegranate, feta and fennel. Garnish with citrus zest and extra mint.
4. Serve piled onto lettuce leaves.

This is a wonderfully refreshing salad with a spicy meal. Juicy, zesty oranges lightly perfumed with rose water and lifted with plenty of fresh mint. Rose water is a much loved ingredient in the Mediterranean, North Africa and the Middle East. We all know the rose water taste in Turkish Delight, but it is equally special in savoury dishes like rose harissa. A bit like vanilla, a little goes a long way. Add juicy Medjool dates and vivid green pistachio nuts and you'll have a gorgeous salad to grace your dinner table.

Orange, Pistachio and Rose Water Salad

SERVES 4 AS A SIDE DISH

Ingredients:

- 6 oranges
- 1-2 T rose water
- Squeeze of lemon juice
- 115g Medjool dates, halved lengthways
- 50g pistachio nuts
- 3 T finely choppped mint
- Icing sugar, to garnish

Method:

1. Peel the oranges with a sharp knife and remove any pith. Slice into very thin half moons. Try to capture the juice and pour into the serving bowl or platter.
2. Arrange the orange slices on a serving platter. Sprinkle over rose water and a squeeze of lemon juice.
3. Scatter over chopped dates and pistachio nuts.
4. Garnish with the finely chopped mint and just before serving, dust over some icing sugar.

Non vegetarians often have the impression that vegetarian food is boring and flavourless. This tagine is anything but: aromatic spices, vibrant vegetables, hearty beans, fresh herbs and citrus makes this a memorable dish. The plant protein in the beans and chickpeas will keep you satieted for longer than a vegetable only recipe. This dish will stay fresh in the fridge for three days-great to bring into work as a packed lunch.

Hearty Vegetable and Bean Tagine

SERVES 4

Ingredients:

- 1 T olive oil
- 2 cloves garlic, crushed
- 1 thumb ginger, grated
- 1 t ground cumin
- 1 t ground coriander
- 1 t caraway seeds
- 1 t turmeric
- ½ t cayenne pepper
- 1 tin chickpeas, rinsed and drained
- 1 tin butterbeans, rinsed and drained
- 1 sweet potato, cubed into bite size pieces
- ½ small head cauliflower, broken into florets
- 1 courgette, sliced into 1.5cm half moons
- 1 tin chopped tomatoes
- 500ml vegetable stock

Garnish

- Juice and zest of 1 lemon
- Juice and zest of 1 orange
- 2 T fresh coriander, chopped
- 2 T fresh parsely, chopped
- 2 T toasted flaked almonds

Method:

1. Using a large pot, gently sauté the onion in the olive oil until softened and translucent.
2. Add the garlic and ginger and stir for 3 minutes.
3. Add the dried spices and stir until fragrant, add a splash of water if you are concerned about burning the spices.
4. Pour in the tomatoes, stock, chickpeas, beans and vegetables.
5. Bring to the boil, cover and reduce to a simmer for 20 minutes until the vegetables are just tender.
6. Lightly toast the flaked almonds in a small pan-do not use any oil.
7. Garnish the tagine with the lemon, orange, coriander, parsely and flaked almonds.
8. Serve with quinoa or couscous to mop up all the sauce.

This is a wonderfully light, fluffy cake due to the airy whisked egg whites folded in. Subtly scented with spices and lightly fragranced with citrus, this cake is perfect with a cup of tea. Or serve as a dessert with Greek yoghurt and fresh fruit if you want a lighter finish to a meal. I've used vanilla bean paste here which is one of my Pantry Pals-I love the aroma and natural sweetness of real vanilla seeds. The solid ingredients in this cake are measured in millilitres, so use your measuring jug instead of weighing scales.

Spiced Citrus Cake

MAKES 1 MEDIUM CAKE

Ingredients:

- 500ml self-raising flour
- 175ml caster sugar
- ½ t salt
- 125ml sunflower oil
- 5 eggs, separated
- 200ml water
- Zest of 1 orange
- Zest of 2 limes
- 1 t vanilla bean paste
- 1 t ground cinnamon
- 2 t butter
- 2 T icing sugar

Method:

1. Sift together the flour, salt and sugar.
2. Add the oil, beaten yolks and cold water, whisk well.
3. Beat the egg white until stiff peaks form and fold into the batter, along with the vanilla, spices and citrus zest.
4. Pour the batter into a large, buttered spring form cake tin and bake at 180°C for about an hour.
5. Allow the cake to cool before removing from the tin.
6. Dust with icing sugar.

Chapter 7

Chineseish

*This is a great takeaway**ish** recipe, all the tastes and textures of a traditional Chinese, but with extra crunch and veggies. Use skinless boneless chicken thighs for really juicy, tender chicken, much better than chicken fillets. You can make this a vegetarian main meal by swopping out the chicken for extra veggies like courgettes and extra peppers. The real **ish** ingredient is pale dry sherry, also called fino sherry. This is the closest Western equivalent to Chinese shaohsing wine which is a traditional rice wine. It makes the sauce really fragrant and authentic. Add water chestnuts and bamboo shoots for even more authenticity. Our Pantry Pal in this recipe is ready to use noodles which are precooked, lightly oiled and vacuum packed. Loosen and add to any stir fry for instant noodley goodness.*

Chow Down Chicken Noodles

SERVES 6

Ingredients:

- 500g skinless boneless chicken thigh or breast fillets, diced into bite size pieces

Marinade:

- 1 T cornflour
- 2 T soy sauce
- 1 T oyster sauce
- 2 t sugar

Vegetables:

- Sunflower oil, for stir frying
- 2 onions, sliced into thin wedges
- 2 cloves garlic, crushed
- 1 T grated ginger
- 1 green pepper, sliced
- 2 celery sticks, diagonally sliced
- 6 spring onions, diagonally sliced
- 150g mushrooms, thinly sliced
- ½ Chinese leaf cabbage, finely shredded
- 300g ready to use noodles

Sauce:

- 4 t cornflour
- 2 T cold water
- 2 T dry sherry
- 250ml chicken stock
- 2 T soy sauce

Method:

1. Combine the chicken, cornflour, soy sauce, oyster sauce and sugar in dish. Cover and refrigerate for 1 hour to marinate the chicken.
2. Heat a little oil in a wok till very hot. Stir fry the chicken in batches for 4-5 minutes until nicely browned and cooked through. Set aside in a clean bowl.
3. Add more oil to the wok and soften the onion. Add the garlic, ginger, green pepper, mushrooms and spring onions and stir fry for 3-4 minutes. Add 2 tablespoons of water to create steam and cook the veggies without the need for more oil.
4. To make the sauce, dissolve the cornflour in the cold water and whisk well. Combine all the sauce ingredients and add to the wok.
5. Add the cabbage and bring to the boil till the sauce thickens and the cabbage begins to wilt.
6. Return the chicken and break in the noodles and heat through.
7. Taste and season to taste. Go easy on the salt as soya sauce and chicken stock are both salty.

This recipe was originally concocted as a tempting and delicious way to prepare tempeh. Tempeh is a traditional soya bean product from Indonesia. Whole soya beans are mixed with a probiotic culture, compressed into little 'bricks' and left to mature. This produces a nutty, savoury flavoured product with an interesting texture. Full of B12 and fibre, this is a great alternative to tofu. Find it in the freeezer of The Hopsack health shop. It's the marinade in this recipe that really rocks, so can be used with chicken and prawns instead.

Sticky Citrusy Prawn Salad

SERVES 4

Ingredients:

- 20-25 large tiger prawns, shelled, headed and deveined
- 1 T sunflower oil
- 6 spring onions, finely sliced
- 8 baby corn cobs, sliced
- 100g bean sprouts
- 2 carrots, peeled into ribbons
- ½ Chinese Cabbage, finely shredded
- 2 T sesame seeds, toasted

***Marinade*:**

- 1 T toasted sesame oil
- 5cm ginger, grated
- 2 clove garlic, crushed
- 10cm lemongrass stalk, grated with a Microplane grater
- Juice of 2 lemons
- 2 T balsamic vinegar
- 2 T maple syrup
- 200ml fresh orange juice
- 100ml soy sauce

Method:

1. Mix all the marinade ingredients together and marinate the prawns for an hour in the fridge.
2. Lift out the prawns and reserve the marinade.
3. Heat up a wok or griddle pan and cook the prawns until they are pink, curled up and firm. This will only take 3 to 5 minutes.
4. Bubble up the marinade in the pan until it goes thick and syrupy.
5. Mix all the vegetables with the cooked prawns and drizzle over the marinade.
6. Garnish with toasted sesame seeds.

After years of teaching and thousands of cookery students, rice is the one dish that causes problems: too wet, too dry, too clumpy, not fluffy, pots boiling over! I'm fortunate that I have a Miele Steam Oven that cooks rice to fluffy perfection, but for many years I cooked my rice the way Natti, a very pretty but very strict Thai lady, taught me. This method only works consistently with basmati rice as most white long grained rice has been parcooked before you buy it, so each brand will vary. This method is not scientific, but just go with it. Many happy students will vouch for its success!

Best Basmati Rice

SERVES 6

Ingredients:

- 2 cups of white basmati rice
- Cold water
- A pinch of salt

Optional aromatics:

- 2 T coconut milk
- 1 red chilli, roughly chopped
- 1 lemongrass stem, bruised
- 1 lime leaf or piece of lime
- 3 slices of fresh ginger

Method:

1. Pour half the rice into a sieve and rinse very well under a cold running tap. The water should run clear. Natti used to make me rinse the rice 8 times! Tip the rinsed rice into a medium sized pot and repeat with the remainding half.
2. Once all the rice is in the pot, it's time to add the water. To measure the amount, rest your hand flat on top of the rice and pour in enough water so that it just covers your hand past the knuckles.
3. Add in the aromatics, if you are using any. Don't use all of them at once, 1 or 2 are sufficient.
4. Cover the pot with a tight fitting lid, this is essential. If your lid is a bit wonky, cover again with foil to trap the steam.
5. Bring the pot to the boil and allow to gather steam for a minute.
6. Switch off and leave for half an hour. DO NOT LIFT THE LID. The steam is cooking the rice and you don't want it to evaporate.
7. After half an hour, fluff up with a fork and discard the aromatics.

*This is a great 'catch all' recipe for the end of the week where you can use up bits of veggies and leftover chicken to make a really tasty, filling meal. And as it is takeaway***ish***, it feels like a treat on a Friday evening. Slice the veggies very finely and once they are stir fried, they will marry together. Our Freezer Friends frozen petis pois and bacon lardons add tasty little nuggets. Our* ***ish*** *factors fresh ginger, soya sauce and toasted sesame oil add* ***ish*** *pizazz to a recipe that can be quite bland. Aim for more veggie and meaty bits and less rice for an interesting, del***ish*** *meal.*

Friday Fried Rice

SERVES 6

Ingredients:

- 400g cooked white or brown rice, either just cooked or completely cold
- 4 eggs, beaten
- Sunflower oil
- 1 T grated ginger or ginger paste
- 6 spring onions, chopped, use white and green
- 250g button mushrooms, sliced
- 6 rashers, diced
- 3 T soy sauce
- ½ cup frozen petis pois
- Few drops toasted sesame oil
- Black pepper

Optional extras:
prawns, cooked chicken, ham, grated carrot, finely sliced cabbage

Method:

1. Heat a teaspoon of oil in a wok. Add the beaten eggs and stir rapidly until well cooked, dry and broken up.
2. Remove the egg from the wok and set aside in a clean bowl.
3. Wipe the wok, heat up 1 tablespoons of oil and cook all the vegetables and meat you want to use.
4. Add the cooked rice and soy sauce. Stir very well and break up any lumps. Add the frozen peas and stir well to defrost, they don't need cooking as such.
5. Once the rice is piping hot, stir through the egg and season with black pepper and sesame oil.
6. For food safety, only reheat once.

*This is a favourite takeaway**ish** recipe, perfect for kids and people trying to convert to healthier dinners. Jam packed with extra crunchy, colourful veggies that you can sneak into your families' diet. The **ish** factor is the sauce, authentic tasting but with a fraction of the sugar of shop bought 'cook in' sauces.*

Sweet and Sour Chicken

SERVES 6

Ingredients:

- 4 chicken breasts, sliced into thin strips and seasoned with salt and pepper
- Sunflower oil, for stir frying
- 1 red onion, sliced into thin wedges
- 1 red pepper, thinly sliced
- 1 yellow pepper, thinly sliced
- 1 green pepper, thinly sliced
- 2 celery sticks, thinly sliced
- 400g tin of pineapple pieces, drained and juice reserved

Sweet and Sour Sauce

- 2 T tomato ketchup
- 2 T plum sauce
- 2 T light soy sauce
- 60ml white wine vinegar
- 1 T cornflour dissolved in 1 T water
- 60ml chicken stock (use a corner of a stock cube)
- Reserved pineapple juice

To serve:
Brown basmati rice

Method:

1. Mix all the sauce ingredients together and set aside.
2. Heat 1 tablespoon of oil in a wok and stir fry the chicken in batches until browned and cooked through. Set aside in a clean bowl.
3. Heat another tablespoon of oil and stir fry the vegetables until cooked but still crunchy, approximately 3 minutes.
4. Add the chicken, pineapple pieces and sauce. Bring to the boil and wait for the sauce to thicken while stirring.
5. Serve immediatley with brown basmati rice.

This is my go to dish when I need a green vegetable side. Steaming the veggies keeps them crunchy and vibrant green. One of my pet peeves are khaki green vegetables. Chinese 5 Spice is an aromatic spice blend with hints of ginger and anise, perfect for seasoning crisp greens. I use a variety of green veggies: asparagus, frozen peas, green beans, broccoli and mangetout.

Five Spiced Steamed Greens

SERVES 4

Ingredients:

- 1 bunch tender stem broccoli, about 12 florets
- 1 courgette, diced into small cubes
- 150g mangetout or sugarsnap peas
- 1 t Chinese 5 Spice
- 2 T olive oil
- Salt and pepper

Method:

1. Steam the vegetables for 3 minutes in a steam oven or a stove top steamer pot.
2. Gently heat the oil, Chinese 5 spice, salt and pepper in a small pan or pot. A minute or two is plenty.
3. Toss vegetables with 5 Spice, olive oil, salt and pepper.

This is one of my number one side dishes and my students and friends agree! Sweet potato is a really nutritious, slow releasing carbohydrate. I prefer steaming potatoes as it retains the vitamins better than boiling them. Sweet potatoes are much softer than regular potatoes and quite moist so they need very little butter to mash. Fresh ginger is the perfect spice to complement the sweetness of the vegetable. This is a very versatile side dish and will go with many different cuisines and dishes.

Ginger Sweet Potato Mash

SERVES 6

Ingredients:

- 6 sweet potatoes, peeled and cubed
- 50g butter
- 1 T honey
- 2 t grated ginger
- Salt and pepper

Method:

1. Steam or boil the sweet potatoes. Drain well.
2. Melt the butter in a pot and gently fry the ginger. Add in the honey and season well.
3. Add the sweet potato to the pot and roughly mash. Adjust the seasoning and serve hot.

*It can be tricky to find a dessert to finish off an Asian meal. Fresh exotic fruit is the ideal choice, but sometimes we want a little decadent touch. This delicious syrup is heavenly, my students go gaga over it. Make extra and keep in a clean screw top jar in the fridge for 2 weeks. Heat up and serve with vanilla ice cream-del**ish**! The **ish** factors are the aromatic spices and lime juice used in the syrup.*

Exotic Fruit Salad with Aromatic Syrup

Ingredients:

- 1 mango, peeled and cubed
- 1 pineapple, peeled and cubed
- 2 kiwi fruit, peeled and sliced
- 1 punnet strawberries, hulled and halved
- 1 tin lychees, drained
- 2 star fruit, sliced
- 500ml Glenisk Greek yoghurt to serve
- 2 T finely chopped mint, to serve

Aromatic syrup:

- 350g caster sugar
- 300ml fresh orange juice
- Juice of 2 limes
- 1 vanilla pod
- 2 star anise
- 5cm of ginger, peeled and sliced
- 2 cardamom pods, bruised
- 2 cinnamon sticks

Method:

1. Boil all the syrup ingredients together until thick and syrupy, be careful not to boil over.
2. Allow to infuse for 10 minutes.
3. Pour warm syrup over the fruit and serve with Greek yoghurt and fresh mint.

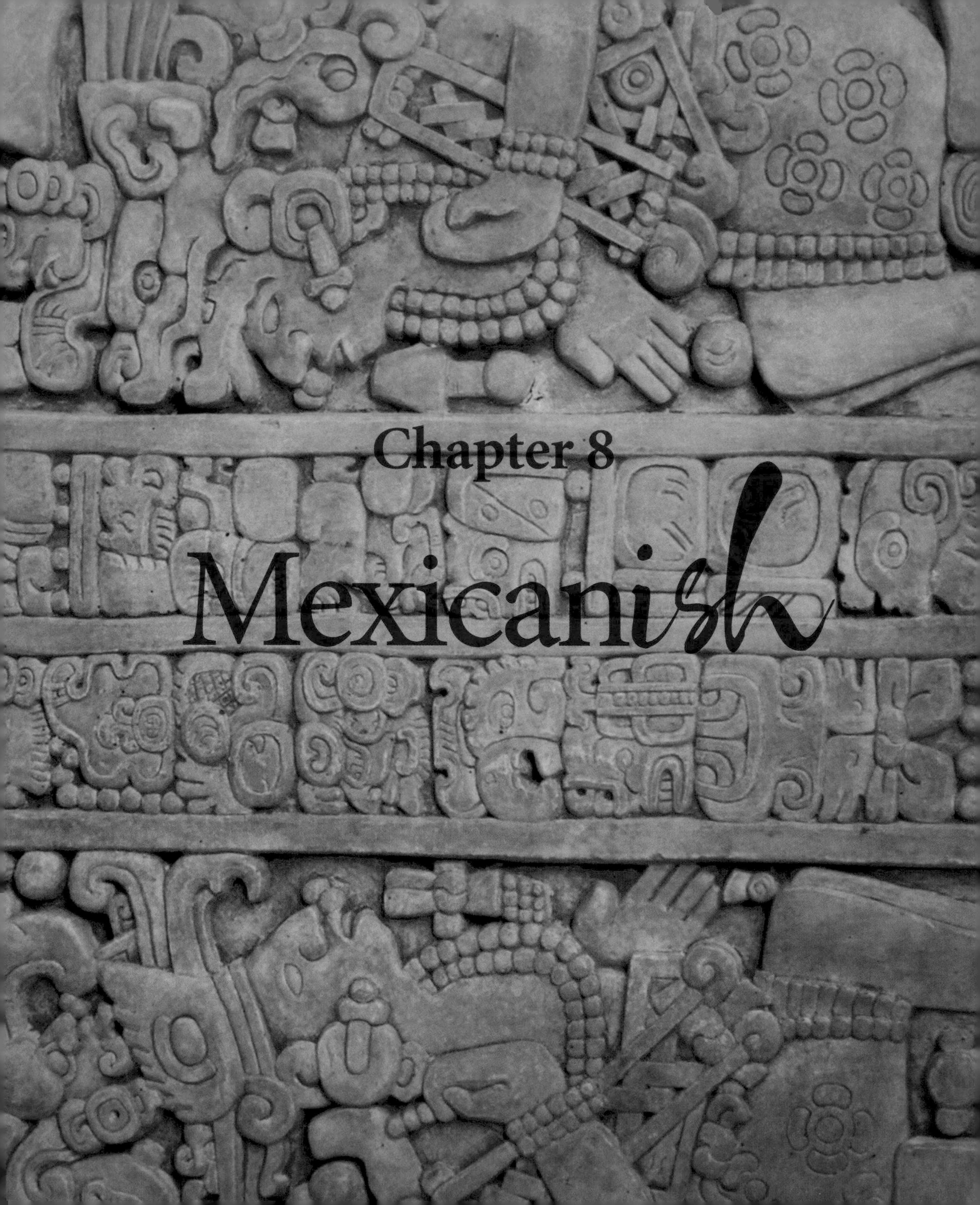

Chapter 8

Mexicanish

This is a very old recipe of mine, and still one of my favourites. Delicious served hot or cold, ideal for brunch or a light lunch. Make a double batch and pack into picnic baskets and lunchboxes. Perfect on its on with the chunky salsa salad or can be served with a grilled tuna steak, simply seasoned with chilli and lime. The trick is to get a good golden colour on the fritters so that the corn is crispy and delicious.

Corn and Courgette Fritters with Salsa Salad

SERVES 4

Ingredients:

- 50g butter, melted
- 125ml milk
- 110g plain flour
- 2 eggs, beaten
- 210g tin sweetcorn, drained
- 2 medium courgette, grated
- Sunflower oil, for frying
- 8 slices Parma ham, grilled or dry fried until crispy

Chunky Salsa Salad

- 3 medium tomatoes, diced
- 2 medium avocados, diced
- 1 small red onion, finely diced
- 2 T lime juice
- 2 T fresh coriander chopped
- Salt and pepper

Method:

1. Mix together the salsa salad and season with salt and pepper. Set aside.
2. Whisk together the milk, eggs, butter and flour until smooth.
3. Stir in the sweetcorn and courgette and mix well.
4. Heat a little oil in a medium hot pan and drop heaped tablespoons of batter onto the pan. Cook for two to three minutes on each side until golden brown.
5. Crisp up the Parma ham under the grill or in a dry frying pan.
6. Drain on absorbent paper then serve with salsa and crispy Parma ham

I concocted this recipe to serve with the Creamy Lime Chicken Enchiladas, but have ended up using it regularly for BBQ's and summer buffets. Even in Winter, it brightens up a table and provides a little tastebud sunshine. If you can't get a fresh papaya, you can buy it tinned. Fresh or tinned mango would also be a good substitute. Likewise, tinned kidney beans can be used instead of black beans. I use sweet and tangy peppadews in the salad instead of chillis. The salad is quite robust and will stay fresh in the fridge for 3 days, bar a little discolouration of the avocado.

Papaya Avocado Salsa Salad

SERVES 6 AS A SIDE DISH

Ingredients:

- 1 tin sweetcorn, rinsed and drained
- 1 tin black beans, rinsed and drained
- 1 papaya, peeled and cubed
- 250g cherry tomatoes, halved
- 6 spring onions, finely chopped
- 2 T chopped peppadews
- Juice and zest of 2 limes
- ½ cup chopped fresh coriander
- 3 avocados
- Salt and pepper

Method:

1. Mix all the ingredients except the coriander and avocado.
2. Just before serving, stir in the coriander.
3. Halve the avocado, remove the stone. Season with salt, pepper and a squeeze of lime. Pile the salad into the cavity of the avo and have it spilling over.

This is a great recipe for a 'braai' or BBQ as the sticky marinade caramalises and gives that distinctive charred BBQ affect. It still works well in the oven, just remember to line the tray! Make up a batch of the marinade and keep in the fridge for up to 2 weeks for emergency sticky chicken cravings. The side dish of pineapple salsa is colourful and contemporary and is an absolute taste sensation.

Sticky Chicken with Pineapple Salsa

8 CHICKEN PIECES (DRUMSTICKS AND THIGHS)

Ingredients:

- 8 chicken pieces (drumsticks and thighs)

Sticky marinade:

- 1 cup tomato paste
- 1 cup Mrs Ball's Peach Chutney
- ¼ cup red wine vinegar
- 2 T brown sugar
- 2 garlic cloves, crushed
- 5 cm fresh ginger, grated
- ½ t chilli powder
- Salt and pepper

Pineapple Salsa:

- 2 cups of pineapple chunks (1 large tin or 1 fresh pineapple)
- ½ red onion, finely diced
- Juice of 2 limes
- ½ red chilli, finely chopped
- 2 T fresh coriander, chopped

Method:

1. In a large bowl, mix all the marinade ingredients together. Put aside one cup of marinade for basting. Toss the chicken in the marinade to coat well, cover and refrigerate for 1 hour.
2. Preheat the oven to 220°C. Line a baking tray with a silicone sheet or baking parchmen. Place a cooling rack onto the baking tray and place the chicken on this. This will allow the hot air to circulate and to caramalise the chicken. Bake for 35-40 minutes until cooked through. Use a silcone brush to baste the chicken with the extra marinade.
3. Mix together the pineapple salsa ingredients and allow the flavours to infuse for 10 minutes.
4. Serve the sticky chicken hot with pineapple salsa.

This is a meaty version of a favourite Mexican classic of mine. Perfect for brunch with a pitcher of Bloody Mary. Or a cure from one too many the night before! Easy enough for kids to make as a breakfast in bed for Fathers' Day. Chorizo, chilli, tomato and poached eggs make for a very hearty meal to warm you up.

Huevos Rancheros

SERVES 4

Ingredients:

- 200g chorizo sausage, chopped into small cubes
- 2 red onions, finely diced
- 1 clove garlic, crushed
- 1 red chilli, finely chopped or 3 peppadews, sliced
- 1 red or green pepper, finely chopped
- 250g cherry tomatoes, halved
- 1 tin chopped tomatoes
- 1 T red wine vinegar
- 1 t sugar
- Salt and pepper
- 8 eggs
- 1 pack corn tortillas

Method:

1. Fry the chorizo in a large frying pan till the fat renders out and the chorizo goes crispy.
2. Add the onion, garlic, chilli and peppers and sauté until softened.
3. Stir in the tomatoes, salt and pepper, sugar and vinegar. Simmer for 10 minutes. Check again for seasoning.
4. Make wells in the tomato mixture and crack the eggs into it. Put a lid over the pan and simmer for 10-15 minutes. Alternatively poach the eggs separately.
5. To toast the tortillas, place them flat in a dry hot pan and toast on both sides.
6. Serve toasted tortillas with the eggs and plenty of spicy sauce.

This is a great recipe for a Meat Free Monday, whether you are one person, two or more. Great fun for kids, as they can mix 'n match and create their own filling combinations. The chickpea base has a wonderful flavour and texture, you wont miss the meat at all! The filling will stay fresh in the fridge for 3 days and makes a super packed lunch. Go easy on the sour cream and grated cheese and you will have a very figure friendly meal.

Chickpea Salsa Wraps

SERVES 4

Ingredients:

- 1 T olive oil
- 1 onion, finely diced
- 1 clove garlic, crushed
- 1 t paprika
- Pinch ground chilli powder
- 1 t cumin
- 400g tomato purée
- 1 tin chickpeas, rinsed and drained
- 2 T coriander, chopped
- 8 corn tortillas
- 1 small red onion, finely diced
- 1 tomato, finely diced
- 1 avocado, diced
- 1 cup grated cheddar cheese
- 1 cup finely shredded iceberg lettuce
- 250ml Glenisk crème fraiche

Method:

1. Cook the onion and garlic in a little olive oil until soft. Stir in the spices for a minute. Add the purée, bring to a boil then reduce to a simmer for 10 minutes.
2. Stir in the chickpeas and simmer for a further 5 minutes.
3. Mix in the fresh coriander and season to taste.
4. Heat up the tortillas in the oven if preferred.
5. Divide the chickpea mixture between the tortillas and add tomato, onion, avocado, cheese, crème fraiche and lettuce.

This recipe uses one of the Freezer Treasures-pink, precooked prawns. They work a treat in this recipe with the fresh flavours of lime, chilli and coriander. Brown rice is a healthy source of fibre and slow release carbohydrates and makes this salad into a complete meal. Lots of bright crunchy veggies will help you towards your five a day. Very substantial and great as a packed lunch. Transport the salad in a little cooler bag for food safety.

Rainbow Brown Rice Salad

SERVES 4

Ingredients:

- 250g pink, precooked prawns
- 1 cup brown basmati or short grain brown rice
- 2 ½ cups water
- 1 red pepper, finely chopped
- 1 green pepper, finely chopped
- 3 tomatoes, finely diced
- 3 spring onions, finely chopped
- 2 celery sticks, finely chopped
- 2 T lemon juice
- 2 T olive oil
- 2 T Glenisk crème fraiche
- 2 T fresh coriander, finely chopped
- salt and pepper

Method:

1. You can either steam the brown rice in a steamer or simmer in a pot. Combine the rice and water in a pot, bring to the boil, then reduce to a simmer with the lid askew until just tender, this will take about 20-25 minutes. If you are using easy cook rice, follow the cooking instruction on the bag.
2. Spread the cooked rice onto a clean tray and fan to cool down. Chill in the fridge for an hour or two. The rice must be completely cold, otherwise you will bread bacteria.
3. Drain the prawns well in a colander if they are in brine.
4. Chop all the veggies very finely, no bigger than the size of the prawns.
5. Mix all the ingredients to combine, season with salt and pepper and garnish with extra coriander.

Make sure to either eat rice hot or chilled. At tepid temperatures it breeds bacteria after 90 minutes.

This recipe was inspired by Bill Clinton's version-before he became a vegan! The creamy, zesty lime chicken filling contrasts really well with the spicy coriander tomato sauce. Add bubbling, golden melted cheese and you're in comfort food heaven. You can moderate the heat to suit your family's tastebuds for a family friend supper. I often use this as an easy entertaining dish served with the Papaya Avocado Salsa Salad. Leftovers taste even better!

Creamy Lime Chicken Enchiladas

SERVES 8

Ingredients:

Creamy Lime Chicken Filling:

- 4 chicken breasts
- 2 bay leaves
- 4 peppercorns
- Pinch of salt
- 1 t cumin seeds
- 3 spring onions, finely chopped
- Juice and zest of 2 limes
- 250ml Glenisk crème fraiche
- 1 t Cajun spice
- 1/2 cup chopped fresh coriander
- Salt and pepper
- 250g mature cheddar, grated
- 8 corn tortillas

Tomato Sauce:

- 2 T olive oil
- 1 red onion, finely chopped
- 2 cloves garlic, crushed
- 1 t ground cumin
- 500ml bottle passata or 1 tin chopped tomatoes
- 1 T tomato paste
- 1 T jalapeno chilli, finely chopped
- Handful of coriander stalks
- 1 t sugar
- Salt and pepper

Method:

1. Bring a large pot of water to the boil. Add the chicken, onion, bay leaves, cumin seeds, salt and pepper. Bring back up to the boil. Reduce to a simmer and poach for 15 minutes. Remove from the poaching liquid and allow to rest for 10 minutes. Shred finely with your fingers.
2. Mix the shredded chicken with the spring onions, lime, crème fraiche, cajun spice and coriander. Taste and season.
3. To make the tomato sauce, heat the oil in a pot and gently fry the onion and garlic until soft. Add the ground cumin and stir briefly till fragrant. Pour in the passata, add the chilli, sugar and coriander stalks. Simmer for 20 minutes. Season with salt and pepper. Blitz to a smooth sauce with a handheld blender.
4. Spoon a little sauce on the bottom of a lasagne dish.
5. Take a tortilla, spoon in some chicken mixture and roll up tightly. Place in the dish. Repeat until all the chicken is used up.
6. Pour over the rest of the sauce. Sprinkle over the cheese. Bake at 180°C for 30 minutes until golden and bubbling.
7. Allow to rest for 5 minutes then serve with Papaya Avocado Salsa Salad.

*Kids love chicken goujons, so I have created a fun and novel Mexican **ish** version of this favourite family meal. Use Cajun or Mexican spice to flavour the chicken, even the little spice packets left over from your Mexican dinner kits! Crème fraiche or sour cream is used instead of egg to coat the chicken. The dippers are crumbed in crushed nachos-great fun and super duper easy! Baked instead of deep fried for a healthier version. Plus a healthy avocado dip instead of mayonnaise.*

Nachos Crusted Chicken Dippers

SERVES 4

Ingredients:

- 4 skinless boneless chicken breasts sliced into 6 pieces
- 2 T Cajun or Mexican spice mix
- 250ml Glenisk crème frache
- 200g nachos, coarsely crushed
- Lime wedges, to served

Avocado dipping sauce:

- 2 avocados, mashed
- Juice of 1 lime
- 1 T Glenisk crème fraiche
- 2 T chopped coriander
- 1 T chopped jalapeno pepper
- Salt and pepper

Method:

1. Coat the chicken pieces evenly in the spice. Dip into the crème fraiche and lightly coat. Finally, roll the chicken dippers in the nachos crumbs.
2. Line a baking tray with parchment paper and rest the dippers in the fridge for at least 10 minutes, this will allow the crumbs to set.
3. Preheat an oven to 220°C and bake the chicken dippers for 10 minutes.
4. Mix together the avocado dip and season with salt and pepper to taste. I love lime so I often add an extra squeeze.
5. Serve the dippers hot with avocado dipping sauce and lime wedges.

I love this mess free, low fat alternative to the traditional toasted sandwich. Simply place a shop bought tortilla on a dry frying pan, top with a filling of your choice, sandwich with another tortilla, toast and flip over. Less fat, no mess and the filling combinations are endless. These fillings are inspired by the many many Cheesey Toasties I've enjoyed in my pals Gerry and Elish's home at 2am in the morning!

Quesadilla Cheesy Toasties

SERVES 8

Ingredients:

Italian*ish:*

Spread a layer of basil pesto onto both tortillas. Arrange a single layer of salami slices on top and add a few chopped sundried or sunblush tomatoes. Sprinkle on a generous amount of grated mozzarella or tear up pieces of buffalo mozzarella.

Span*ish:*

Spread a layer of tomato or red pepper relish on both tortillas. Arrange a single layer of chorizo slices on top and add some chopped peppadews and finely chopped spring onions. Sprinkle on a generous amount of grated manchego cheese or strong cheddar.

Greek*ish:*

Spread a thin layer of black olive tapenade onto both tortillas. Wilt some baby leaves spinach by heating a little olive oil in a pan and stirring handfuls of the spinach in till wilted. Squeeze out the moisture and spread onto the tortilla, season with grated nutmeg. Add some crumbled feta cheese.

French*ish:*

Mix a little Dijon mustard with mayonnaise and spread this onto both tortillas. Add some chopped ham and one finely chopped spring onion. Sprinkle on a generous amount of grated Gruyére cheese or strong cheddar.

Tuna Mayo*ish:*

Mix 1 tin of tuna with 2 tablespoons mayonnaise, finely chopped spring onions, juice of 1 lime, chopped coriander, salt and pepper. Spread onto a tortilla and sprinkle on cheese.

Method:

1. Heat a large, heavy pan. Place one tortilla flat on the hot pan. Sprinkle with cheese and whatever other toppings you fancy.
2. Place another tortilla on top. Cook for a minute or two till toasted.
3. When the cheese starts to melt, turn the whole quesadilla over and cook the other side.
4. Cut into wedges and serve with a dip if you fancy.

Churros, also known as the Mexican doughnut, are deep fried cylindrical shaped pastries. These are often served with cinnamon sugar and a chocolate dunking sauce. I don't like deep fried foods, so I have adapted good old fashioned French toast and given it a churros ***ish*** *twist. I've added a bit of orange to complement the cinnamon and chocolate. An ooey gooey messy dessert, great fun for kids to make-chocolate everywhere!*

Churros French Toast Fingers

SERVES 4

Ingredients:

- 4 slices white bread, crusts removed
- 2 eggs
- 150ml milk
- 55g butter
- Sunflower oil
- 2 T granulated sugar
- ½ t ground cinnamon

Chocolate Orange Sauce

- 150g good quality dark chocolate
- 150ml Glenisk cream
- Zest of 1 orange

Method:

1. To make the chocolate sauce, place a glass bowl over a pot of simmering water. Gently melt the chocolate with half the orange zest in the glass bowl. Gradually add the cream and stir well until glossy and smooth. Serve in a warmed jug with extra orange zest for garnish.
2. Cut each slice of bread into 4 fingers.
3. Beat the eggs and milk together in a pie dish or soup plate.
4. Dip the bread fingers into the eggy mixture and coat well.
5. Melt half the butter with a tablespoon of oil in a non stick frying pan. When the butter is foaming, fry the bread until golden brown on both sides. Add the remaining butter and more oil if needed until all the bread is fried.
6. Mix the sugar and cinnamon together and sprinkle over the warm toast.
7. Serve warm with the warm orange chocolate sauce.

Chapter 9

Greekish

A simplified version of traditional Greek spanakopita, these spinach purses are perfect on a meze platter, as a starter or served as a light lunch with salad. Filo pastry can be tricky to use as it can dry out. Keep the unused pastry covered with a damp cloth while you work. And make sure every sheet gets a light brushing of butter to help it go cripsy. Raisins and pine nuts give extra interest to the spinach and feta combo. Very moreish.

Spinach Purses

MAKES 12

Ingredients:

- 1 T olive oil
- 1 onion, finely diced
- 2 cloves garlic
- 500g baby spinach leaves
- 1/2 t ground nutmeg
- 150g feta cheese, cubed
- 2 T plump raisins or sultanas
- 2 T pinenuts, toasted
- 3 eggs, whisked
- 80g butter, melted
- 6 sheets filo pastry

Method:

1. Sauté the onion and garlic in a pan until softened.
2. Add the nutmeg and stir until fragrant.
3. Add handfuls of spinach to the pot and stir until just wilted, do not overcook. Drain off any liquid.
4. Mix the spinach with the eggs, cheese, pinenuts and raisins.
5. Preheat the oven to 200°C. Brush a 12 hole muffin tray with a little melted butter.
6. Brush each sheet of filo pastry with butter, cut into 6 squares and layer up, overlapping at an angle in each muffin hole so each hole has at least 4 layers of pastry.
7. Bake the filo pastry cases in the muffin tray for 8 minutes until lightly golden.
8. Divide the spinach mixture between each muffin hole and bake for a further 5-7 minutes.

In a nutshell, kofta are spiced 'meatballs' that are shaped directly onto skewers and BBQ'd or grilled. For this recipe I have used lamb, a favourite in Greek cuisine. The ***ish*** *factor is a wonderful lemony spice-sumac-that complements almost any meat. Serve the kofta stuffed into pita pockets with yoghurt and mint dressing, tomato and lettuce. Great picnic or casual family food. Or even a posh packed lunch!*

Lamb Kofta in Pitta Pockets

SERVES 6

Ingredients:

Lamb Kofta:

- 500g lamb mince
- 1 onion, grated
- 2 cloves garlic, crushed
- Zest of 1 lemon
- 1 t ground cumin
- 1 t ground coriander
- 1 t sumac (a Middle Eastern spice available in Asian markets)
- 2 T finely chopped mint
- 12 metal or bamboo skewers or rosemary branches

Tzatziki (Greek yoghurt and mint sauce)

- 1x500g tub Glenisk Greek yoghurt
- 2 T finely chopped mint
- 1 cucumber, peeled and seeded
- Juice of 1 lemon
- 2 cloves garlic, crushed
- Pinch salt

To serve:

- 12 pita pockets
- 1 iceburg lettuce, finely sliced
- 250g cherry tomatoes, halved
- 1 red onion, finely sliced

Method:

1. Preheat the oven to 230°C or use a BBQ.
2. Mix the kofta mixture well together. Mold onto skewers or rosemary branches in sausage shapes. Cook on the BBQ until golden or place on a rack in the oven for 20 minutes.
3. To make the tzatziki, grate the peeled and seeded cucumber. Place the grated cucumber in a clean teatowel and wring out the moisture. Mix the cucumber with the Greek Yoghurt, lemon juice, mint, salt and garlic.
4. If preferred, heat up the pita pockets and slice open on one side. Place the skewer inside the pocket and pull the kofta off the skewer.
5. Delicious stuffed into a pita pocket with tomatoes, crispy lettuce and the tzatziki.

This is a modern way to use familiar Greek ingredients: aubergine, feta cheese, spinach and almonds. It is worthwhile investing in a griddle pan so that you can toast the bread and griddle the aubergine slices. The smoky, charred effect can't be beat! A healthy veggie option for a light lunch or a thinner dinner.

Grilled Aubergine and Feta Sandwich

SERVES 4 AS A LIGHT LUNCH

Ingredients:

- 8 slices of sourdough bread or baguette
- 2 aubergines, thinly sliced lengthways
- 100g baby spinach leaves
- 200g feta cheese, thinly sliced

Mint pesto:

- 2 cups of mint leaves
- 50g whole blanched almonds, lightly toasted
- 1 clove garlic, crushed
- Juice 1 lemon
- 3 T olive oil

Method:

1. For the pesto, blitz everything in a food processor. If you prefer a thinner consistency, thin down with olive oil. Season to taste with salt, pepper and lemon juice.
2. Heat up a griddle pan. Lightly brush the bread with olive oil and toast both sides on the griddle pan.
3. Brush the aubergine slices with olive oil, season and griddle until tender and charred on both sides.
4. To assemble, spread a little pesto on each slice of bread, top with spinach leaves, feta slices, grilled aubergine and more pesto.
5. Drizzle with olive oil and lemon juice and serve immediately.

My moms' Oregano Crouton Green Beans are the inspiration for this recipe. A combination of thinly sliced veggies marinated in a herby dressing and served with cayenne pepper croutons. The colours, textures and flavours are interesting and vibrant. A real taste of the Mediterranean, but with a modern twist. The sauce in particular is delish, and can be served with fish or chicken.

Herby Marinated Vegetable Salad

SERVES 4

Ingredients:

- 6 baby courgettes, thinly sliced
- 150g button mushrooms, wiped clean and sliced
- 1 red pepper, thinly sliced
- 100g green beans, trimmed and sliced into 2cm lengths
- 100g cherry tomatoes, halved
- 3 spring onions, finely chopped
- 200g feta cheese, crumbled

Cayenne pepper croutons:

- 6 slices of bread, cubed
- 2 T olive oil
- ¼ t cayenne pepper

Herby dressing:

- 2 T baby capers
- 8 black olives, pitted
- 8 green olives, pitted
- ½ cup flat leaf parsley
- 1 clove garlic, crushed
- ½ cup extra virgin olive oil
- ½ cup chopped basil
- ½ cup chopped mint
- ½ cup red wine vinegar

Method:

1. Steam or blanch the green beans for 3 minutes. Refresh in iced water to retain their colour and crunch. Drain well in a colander.
2. Mix the bread cubes with the olive oil. Spread out on a lined baking tray. Sprinkle over the cayenne pepper. Bake at 200°C for 8-10 minutes until golden and crispy. Set aside.
3. Blitz all the dressing ingredients together in a food processor until well blended.
4. Slice and dice the courgettes, mushrooms, tomatoes, spring onions and red pepper. Mix in the green beans.
5. Toss the vegetables and dressing together until well combined. Arrange on a large platter. Crumble over the feta cheese. Garnish with the crispy croutons.

My brother André is the natural gourmand in our family, effortlessly putting ingredients together to create superb meals. After visiting Greece in his early twenties, André came back with a passion for Greek cuisine: rosemary infused lamb, crunchy salads and lots and lots of lemon! As a long distance runner, Greek cuisine is a healthy lifestyle choice for André. Just not too much baklava and shortbread!

André's Halloumi, Peach and Chilli Salad

SERVES 6

Ingredients:

- 2 blocks of halloumi cheese, sliced into 1.5cm pieces
- 6 peaches, halved and stoned
- 2 red chillies, halved lengthways and seeded
- 150g baby salad leaves
- 2 small bulbs of fennel, finely sliced
- Juice of 1 lemon
- 2 T finely chopped mint
- Light olive oil, for cooking

Dressing:

- 250ml Glenisk Greek yoghurt
- Juice of 1 lemon
- 2 T finely chopped mint

Method:

1. Mix the dressing and check for seasoning. Add more lemon if desired. Set aside and allow the flavours to infuse.
2. Marinate the fennel in the juice of one lemon and a drizzle of olive oil.
3. In a pan or on the BBQ, lightly grill the peaches until just golden. If using a pan, use a little light olive oil to cook the peaches in. If cooking on a BBQ, lightly coat the peaches with olive oil before placing on the BBQ grill. Set aside.
4. Repeat with the chillies, pushing them down with tongs to ensure even cooking. Once the chillies start to blister and soften, remove and set aside. Allow to cool slightly before chopping into very thin slices.
5. Using more olive oil, cook the halloumi on both sides until golden brown. Remove and keep warm on a warm plate or in a moderate oven.
6. Gently toss together the fennel and baby salad leaves with a little dressing. Divide between six starter plates or arrange on one large salad platter.
7. Nestle the peaches on the bed of greens, add the halloumi cheese and scatter over the chillies and extra mint.
8. Serve immediately with extra dressing on the side.

Traditionally made with lamb or beef mince, and layered with slices of aubergine and potato, moussaka has always been one of my favourites. Here I have used lentils for a vegetarian version and a special cheesey sauce instead of a bechamél. The texture and flavour of the lentils work brilliantly in this recipe, students often prefer this version! Perfect family food for a Meat Free Monday.

Lovely Lentil Moussaka

SERVES 4

Ingredients:

- 4 medium potatoes, peeled
- 4 large aubergines, thinly sliced lengthways

Lentil mix:

- 1 onion, finely diced
- 1 clove garlic, crushed
- 250g brown lentils
- 750ml vegetable stock
- 2 T red wine or red wine vinegar
- 6 T tomato paste
- A pinch of ground cinnamon
- 2 T fresh parsley, chopped

Cheesy sauce:

- 4 T ricotta cheese
- 4 T Glenisk Greek yoghurt
- 3 eggs
- 4 T finely grated Parmesan cheese
- Fresh nutmeg

Method:

1. To cook the lentils, heat up a little olive oil in a pot. Gently sauté the onion until soft. Stir in the garlic and cook for 2 minutes. Add in the lentils, stock, wine, tomato paste and cinnamon. Bring to a boil then reduce to a simmer, uncovered, for 30 minutes. Stir in the parsley and season with salt and pepper.
2. To prepare the potatoes, steam or boil whole for 25 to 30 minutes until just tender. Allow to cool, then thinly slice and set aside for assembly later.
3. To prepare the aubergines, slice lengthways into 1.5 cm thick slices. Lightly brush with olive oil. Spread out on a baking tray and bake at 200°C for 10 to 15 minutes until golden and starting to char. Set aside.
4. For the cheesy sauce, whisk together the ricotta, Greek yoghurt, eggs and half the Parmesan cheese.
5. Begin assembling by spreading half the lentil mix in the bottom of a lasagne style baking dish. Arrange a layer of potato slices on top, then aubergine slices. Spoon over the rest of the lentil mixture. Layer the remainding aubergine slices and finish off with a layer of potato.
6. Spoon over the cheesy sauce, making sure not to leave any gaps. Sprinkle over the rest of the cheese. Grate over fresh nutmeg.
7. Bake at 200°C for 20 minutes until golden and bubbling.

*If there is lamb shank on the menu, my dad is guaranteed to order it, one of his favourites. And if there is one thing Norman knows how to cook, it's lamb. My dad taught me to make little incisions in the meat and insert slivers of garlic and fresh rosemary to infuse flavour. Cooked low and slow, lamb shank should fall off the bone and melt in your mouth. Served here with a chunky tomato stew for an easy side. The citrusy herby topping is like a gremolata used in Italian cuisine that adds freshness and flavour. So both Greek**ish**, Italian**ish** and Norman**ish**!*

Norman's Braised Lamb Shanks with Chunky Tomato Stew

SERVES 4

Ingredients:

- 4 lamb shanks
- 2 T pure olive oil
- 5 cloves of garlic, peeled and sliced
- 4 sprigs of fresh rosemary
- 4 medium carrots, roughly chopped
- 4 sticks of celery, roughly chopped
- 1 large onion, roughly chopped
- 2 bay leaves
- 12 peppercorns
- 1 bottle of good red wine

Chunky tomato stew:

- 1 T olive oil
- 1 red onion, finely diced
- 2 sticks celery, large diced
- 2 medium carrots, large diced
- 2 tins chopped tomatoes
- 1 T tomato paste
- 1 t sugar
- 1 tin butter beans, rinsed and drained
- Salt and pepper

Citrusy minty topping:

- Zest of 1 orange
- Zest of 1 lemon
- 2 T parsley, chopped
- 2 T mint, chopped
- 2 cloves garlic, sliced

Method:

1. Prepare the lamb shanks by making 6 tiny incisions into each one with a sharp knife to create tiny cavities. Push a sliver of garlic and a few rosemary leaves into these incisions. Season the lamb shanks very well with sea salt and black pepper.
2. Preheat the oven to 150°C. In a large enamelled cast-iron casserole dish, heat the olive oil. Brown the lamb shanks on all 3 sides over a high heat, about 4 minutes per side. Add the carrots, celery and onion to the casserole. Pour in the red wine and boil for 3 minutes. Add the bay leaves and peppercorns. Cover the casserole tightly and transfer to the oven. Braise the lamb shanks, turning once, for 3 hours until tender.
3. To make the chunky tomato stew, heat the olive oil in a pot. Add in the onion, celery and carrot. Place a circle of parchment paper on top of the veggies to trap the steam. Cook on a low heat for 10 minutes, stirring occasionally. Add the garlic and cook for 2 minutes before adding the tomato, tomato paste, balsamic vinegar and sugar. Season with salt and pepper. Bring to a boil, then reduce to a simmer for 30 minutes. Add in the butter beans for the last 10 minutes of cooking. Taste and adjust the seasoning.
4. Mix the citrusy herb topping together and set aside.
5. Make a 'bed' of chunky tomato stew on each dinner plate. Arrange the lamb shanks on top. Drizzle over a little of the cooking liquid, but discard the cooking veggies, they have done their job. Garnish each lamb shank with the citrusy minty topping.

Feta cheese, a traditional Greek cheese made from sheeps' or goats' milk is a staple in my fridge. Low fat, salty and fresh, I use it in a myriad recipes. Here I have taken it up a notch and marinated the feta in lemon, garlic, chilli and herbs. Served with a salad of cucumber,tomato, pistachios and mint, this salad looks spectacular and tastes fantastic. Great for entertaining friends or a relaxed lunch at home, this is Greece on a platter.

Minty Marinated Feta Salad

SERVES 4

Ingredients:

Marinated feta cheese:

- 400g feta cheese, diced into cubes
- 4 cloves garlic, crushed
- ½ red chilli, very finely chopped
- 2 t dried oregano
- 2 t dried mint
- 1 t pink peppercorns, crushed in a mortar and pestle
- 2 bay leaves
- Juice and zest of 1 lemon
- 1 t sugar
- 1 cup extra virgin olive oil

Salad:

- 250g cherry tomatoes, halved
- 1 cucumber, diced into cubes
- 100g kalamata olives
- 100g pistachio nuts, lightly crushed
- ½ red onion, very finely sliced
- 1 lemon
- 1 cup finely shredded mint leaves
- 4 pita breads
- Extra lemons

Method:

1. Mix all the ingredients together for the marinade. Place the feta cheese in a bowl and pour over the marinade. Give the bowl a good shake to distribute the marinade, do not stir as this will break up the cheese. Leave to marinate for at least 1 day before eating.
2. Very finely slice the red onion and squeeze over the juice of half a lemon, allow to 'pickle' for 10 minutes.
3. Dice the cucumber and halve the cherry tomatoes. Mix these with the pistachio nuts and kalamata olives. Squeeze over the juice of half a lemon. Season with salt and pepper. Lift the onion out of the lemon juice and mix through the salad. Scatter over the fresh mint leaves.
4. Lightly toast the pita pockets.
5. Arrange a platter or four plates with salad and toasted pita pockets. Lift the feta out of the marinade and spoon over the salad, drizzle with the marinade.
6. Squeeze over more lemon if desired and garnish with lemon zest.

I adore quinoa and serve it at least once a week in some shape or form. A gluten free, high protein grain from South America, quinoa is not only super nutritious but super versatile. It has a wonderful, slightly nutty flavour and soaks up sauce very well. The flavour is fairly neutral, so I use it across cuisines and serve it as a side with curries, tagines and casseroles. Perfect as a filling base for a wholesome, balanced main meal. Here it makes a traditional Greek salad more substantial.

Quinoa Greek Salad

SERVES 4 AS A SIDE DISH

Ingredients:

- 1 cup quinoa
- 2 cups stock
- 4 T olive oil
- Juice of 2 lemons
- 1 cucumber, diced into cubes
- 4 large tomatoes, diced
- 100g kalamata olives
- 3 spring onions, finely chopped
- 1cup of parsley, finely chopped
- ½cup mint, finely chopped
- 100g feta cheese, crumbled

Method:

1. Place the quinoa in a pot with the two cups of stock. Bring to the boil then reduce to a simmer for 15 minutes until the liquid is gone and the quinoa has unravelled.
2. Fluff up the quinoa with a fork and dress with olive oil, lemon juice, salt and pepper. Adjust the flavours and add more olive oil and lemon juice if you prefer.
3. Mix through the herbs, spring onions, tomatoes, cucumber and olives. Crumble over the feta.
4. Will keep fresh in the fridge for 3 days, bar some discolouration of the herbs.

Figs to me epitomise Ancient Greece, so I couldn't have a Greek chapter without featuring figs. This is a very easy, bung it all together cake that is ready in no time. The figs bake into the sponge to become sticky and melt in the mouth. The pistachio orange syrup is reminiscent of baklava and a good dollop of Greek yoghurt finishes it off.

Fig Cake with Orange Blossom Water

MAKES 1 LOAF

Ingredients:

- 170g flour
- 1 ½ t baking powder
- 220g caster sugar
- 125g melted butter
- 2 eggs
- 125ml milk
- 1 T orange blossom water
- 6 fresh figs

Pistachio Orange Syrup:

- 100g pisatchio nuts, roughly crushed
- 100ml honey
- Zest of 1 orange
- Glenisk Greek yoghurt, to serve

Method:

1. Preheat the oven to 180° C
2. Mix together all the ingredients for the loaf except the figs. Whisk until smooth and lump free.
3. Grease a small loaf tin and pour the mixture in.
4. Halve the figs and push them into the cake batter.
5. Bake for 40 minutes until just cooked through but still moist.
6. Leave to cool slightly in the loaf tin for 10 minutes before turning out.
7. Heat up the syrup and pour over the still warm cakes before serving.
8. Serve warm with a big dollop of Greek yoghurt.

Chapter 10

Spanish

I remember as a little girl watching my big brother Tremaine peel and devein prawns with great expertise. Tremaine is the seafood fundi in our family and does a mean fish 'braai' (BBQ). Probably the most impressive thing is the way he skins and fillets fresh fish-even using a pair of pliers! This is one of his sharing recipes: sauce soaked crusty bread, good friends and lipsmacking noises. Don't be alarmed at the amount of butter and olive oil-it's for dunking the bread.

Tremaine's Chilli Lemon Prawn Salad

SERVES 4

Ingredients:

- 1kg raw tiger prawns, shelled and deveined
- 6 cloves garlic, crushed
- 2 red chillies, finely chopped
- 250g butter
- 250ml mild olive oil
- Juice of 1 lemon
- Salt and pepper
- 400g baby spinach leaves
- 1 red onion, finely sliced
- 250g cherry tomatoes, halved
- 3 T chopped fresh parsley
- 1 loaf French bread

Method:

1. Melt the butter, oil, garlic and chilli together in a large pan. Season with salt and pepper.
2. Add the prawns to the pan and cook until pink and curled.
3. Mix the spinach leaves, red onion and tomatoes in a salad bowl.
4. With a slotted spoon, spoon the prawns over the salad, drizzle with a little sauce. Squeeze lemon juice over. Garnish with parsley.
5. Serve the rest of the sauce in a bowl with the crusty bread.

*This is one of my favourite recipes- it looks really fun and the flavour combination is really more***ish.** *I have had students get up in the middle of the night to eat the leftovers of this recipe! In fairness, it's still del***ish** *cold and makes a great packed lunch. Use really miniature pumpkins to make this as a starter portion or the bulbous part of a butternut squash. If you use a bigger pumpkin, just slice it up into wedges, top with filling and serve with quinoa to mop up the sauce.*

Baked Filled Pumpkin

SERVES 4

Ingredients:

- 2 small butternut squash or miniature pumpkins
- 225g baby spinach leaves
- 2 T sunblush tomatoes
- 100g feta cheese
- 100g chorizo sausage, fried
- 1 tin of chickpeas, drained and rinsed
- Salt and pepper
- Fresh nutmeg

Method:

1. Wrap the butternut squash or pumpkin in foil. Place on a baking tray and bake at 180°C until just tender. This could take anything from 20 to 45 minutes. Check by prodding with a dinner knife.
2. Fry the chorizo until crispy, add the chickpeas, sunblush tomatoes and spinach and heat through.
3. Slice the 'lid' off the pumpkin or cut the bulbous part of the butternut in half. Scrape out all the seeds very well.
4. Spoon in the filling and sprinkle with feta cheese.
5. Replace the 'lid'.

I don't think you can ever have enough interesting veggie and salad recipes. Such as these roasted vegetables which are easy to prepare and versatile to use. Serve with quinoa or couscous for a vegetarian main meal, add handfuls of rocket or baby spinach for a warm salad, or simply serve with crusty bread. Sherry vinegar can be a little tricky to find, but makes a wonderful dressing and gives this real ***ish*** *pizazz. It wont go off quickly, so it's a good Pantry Pal.*

Warm Pepper, Rosemary and Olive Salad

SERVES 4 AS SIDE DISH

Ingredients:

- 3 red peppers, seeded and sliced into strips
- 3 yellow peppers, seeded and sliced into strips
- 2 red onions, sliced into wedges
- 6 cloves of garlic, thinly sliced
- 250g cherry tomatoes
- 50g black olives
- 1 t soft light brown sugar
- 4 T sherry vinegar
- 4 rosemary sprigs
- 2 T olive oil
- Salt and pepper

Method:

1. Preheat the oven to 200°C.
2. Seed the peppers and cut into strips.
3. Mix together the peppers, onion, olives, sugar, garlic and tuck in the rosemary sprigs. I like to rub the rosemary sprigs between my hands first to release the oils. Coat with olive oil, season and mix well.
4. Spread out in a baking dish and roast for 20 minutes.
5. Pour over the sherry vinegar and tuck in the cherry tomatoes. Roast for a further 5 to 10 minutes until the tomatoes soften.
6. Serve hot with crusty bread, quinoa or couscous. Or cold as a salad or stuffed into a tortilla wrap.

This is an incredibly simple tapas style dish that can be rustled up in minutes. Peppadews are native to South Africa-a cross between a chilli and a sweet red pepper. They can be bought in jars preserved in a pickle liquid, and you can choose between mild and hot varieties. Chorizo freezes very well, so the only fresh ingredients you need are fresh parsley, garlic and bread.

Crispy Chorizo and Peppadews

SERVES 6 AS A TAPAS

Ingredients:

- 400g chorizo sausage
- 4 cloves garlic, thinly sliced
- 3 T halved peppadews
- 2 T chopped flat-leaf parsley

Method:

1. Skin and slice the chorizo sausage into half inch slices.
2. Fry in a medium pan until the fat renders out, then crank up the heat to crisp up the chorizo.
3. Add the garlic and peppadews and cook for a further 2 minutes.
4. Garnish with parsley and serve with crusty bread.

This is one of my most successful vegetarian **ish** *recipes. It doesn't always work taking a seafood or meat based recipe and turning it veggie. But in this case, the wonderful Spanish flavours of saffron, tomato, garlic and olives translates really well. Short grain brown rice adds extra fibre and texture without feeling too 'virtuous'. Fresh green beans and toasted pumpkin seeds add crunch and colour. For the die hard meat eaters, this is lovely served with a fillet of simply baked firm white fish or a tuna steak.*

Garden Paella

SERVES 4

Ingredients:

- 1 T olive oil
- 1 onion, finely chopped
- 2 garlic cloves, crushed
- 200g short grain brown rice
- 6 strands saffron
- 600ml vegetable stock
- 1 t dried thyme
- 1 t dried oregano
- 6 tomatoes, skinned and chopped
- 12 black or green olives, chopped
- 6 artichoke hearts, halved
- 115g frozen peas
- 115g green beans, chopped into short lengths
- 2 T chopped fresh parsley
- Juice of 1 lemon
- 2 T pumpkin seeds, toasted
- Black pepper

Method:

1. Add the saffron to the stock and bring to the boil.
2. Heat a little oil in a pan and sauté the onion and garlic until soft.
3. Add the rice and stir for a minute.
4. Pour in the stock, dried herbs, olives, artichoke hearts and chopped tomatoes.
5. Simmer covered for 25 minutes until the rice is cooked, stirring often. Add a little more liquid if necessary.
6. Add the green beans, peas and parsley and cook for a further 5 minutes.
7. Season with lemon and black pepper. Garnish with toasted pumpkin seeds.

I love a good meatball, especially when it's been **ished**. *Our* **ish** *factor, chorizo sausage, comes in two forms:the dried cured sausage like an Italian salami or the raw sausages that you have to cook. For this recipe you are looking for the raw sausages or any good spicy pork sausage. Be careful with the paprika, good quality smoked paprika can be very pungent and packs quite a punch! This recipe is very versatile: serve with wild rice, couscous, mashed potato or even stuffed into tortilla's with tomato, lettuce and sour cream.*

Spicy Spanish Meatballs

SERVES 6

Ingredients:

- 500g lean beef mince
- 500g spicy sausage (I use Hick's Hot and Spicy Sausages)
- 1 onion, grated
- 2 cloves garlic, crushed
- 1 egg, lightly beaten
- 1 cup breadcrumbs
- 1 T smoked paprika
- Few drops Tabasco sauce
- 1 T chopped fresh parsley or 1 t dried mixed herbs
- Salt and pepper

Method:

1. Preheat an oven to 220°C. Line a baking tray with parchment paper.
2. Mix all the ingredients together with your hands. Form into small golf ball size balls and place on the baking tray.
3. Bake for 15 too 20 minutes until cooked through, do not over cook.
4. Serve with a rich tomato sauce and wild rice or spicy rice.
5. The cooked meatballs will freeze for up to 1 month.

This is loosely based on the classic 'patatas bravas' to which I've added tuna and cheese. It reminds me of the rather naff but really tasty tuna pasta bake that was popular in my childhood. I was introduced by a foodie friend, Gerry, to Ortiz Tuna, a Spanish brand of tinned tuna packed in olive oil. It is so good I have been known to eat it with a fork straight from the tin! It is twice the price of the regular brands, but a totally different taste and texture. Thanks Gerry!

Tuna Tomato Potato Bake

SERVES 6

Ingredients:

- 1kg new potatoes, halved
- 3 T olive oil
- 1 onion, finely chopped
- 1 red chilli, finely chopped
- 2 garlic cloves, crushed
- 1 green pepper, diced
- 2 T tomato paste
- 2 tins chopped tomatoes
- 1 T red wine vinegar
- 1 t paprika
- Salt and pepper
- 2 T flat leaf parsley
- 2 tins tuna, drained
- 100g strong cheese like Manchego or cheddar, grated

Method:

1. Steam or boil the potatoes for 10 minutes until just under cooked, drain well in a colander.
2. Heat the oil in a large pan and gently fry the onion and chilli until soft, add the garlic and green pepper and cook for a further 3 minutes.
3. Add in the tomato paste, paprika, vinegar and chopped tomatoes and simmer for 5 minutes.
4. Mix the potatoes, parsely and tuna with the sauce. Taste and season with salt and pepper.
5. Pour into a baking dish, sprinkle over the cheese and bake at 200°C for 20 minutes until golden and bubbling.

I love squid served calamari style-battered, deep fried with chips and tartar sauce. This recipe, however, is a much healthier option. Baby squid can be difficult to find so I often use frozen baby squid from the Asian market or my fishmonger. The freshness is preserved by freezing, plus baby squid is often more tender than the big squid tubes. Squid cooks in seconds, so avoid overcooking or you'll end up with rubber bands-not pleasant.

Baby Squid, Chorizo and Cherry Tomato Salad

SERVES 6 AS A TAPAS

Ingredients:

- 200g chorizo, skinned and thinly sliced
- 2 cloves garlic, crushed
- 8 peppadews, cut into strips
- 4 baby squid, cleaned and cut into rings
- 250g cherry tomatoes, halved
- 200g rocket
- 2 T fresh parsley, to garnish
- Crusty bread, to serve
- Lemon wedges, to serve

Method:

1. Defrost the baby squid in a colander under cold water, this will take about 20 minutes.
2. To clean, pull out the cartilage 'quill' inside, scoop out the insides and wash very well. Remove the head and tentacles if attached. Pull off as much of the purple outer membrane from the tube as possible. Slice the tubes from left to right into 1.5cm slices to form rings. Wash very well in cold water.
3. Cook the chorizo on a medium heat in a large pan until crispy and the fat has rendered out,
4. Add in the garlic and peppadews. Add one tablespoon of the peppadew pickling juice. Season with salt and pepper. Cook for ten minutes on a low heat.
5. Turn up the heat, add in the calamari rings and cherry tomatoes and stir well for 2 minutes until the calamari turns opaque. DO NOT OVERCOOK!
6. Garnish with parsley and serve with plenty of rocket and lemon wedges.

Growing up on a citrus farm in Patensie, South Africa, I remember my mom clipping out newspaper and magazine recipes, especially ones using oranges, lemons and 'naartijies' (mandarins). This is a very old recipe and the ultimate comfort pudding served with cream or custard. It looks pretty weird as you make it, as you pour together hot orange sauce and the sponge batter. But somehow, magic happens in the oven, the two separate and you have a golden orange sponge on top and a thick layer of orange sauce underneath. The Seville orange marmalade, fresh orange juice and zest add a tangy citrusy bite. Don't blame me if you scoff half a pudding on your own!

Monica's Saucy Orange Pudding

SERVES 4

Method:

- 100g butter
- 2 eggs
- 1 T Seville orange marmalade
- 2 t orange zest
- 1 t bread soda
- 250ml milk
- 200g plain flour

Syrup:

- 400ml orange juice
- 50g sugar
- 2 T butter
- Pinch salt

Method:

1. Preheat the oven to 190°C. Grease or butter 1 medium oven proof glass dish or 4 small glass dishes.
2. Cream together the butter, sugar, egg, apricot jam and orange zest together.
3. Dissolve the bread soda in the milk.
4. Add the milk and cake flour alternatively to the sugar mixture, mixing well.
5. Bring all the syrup ingredients to the boil in a saucepan on the hob.
6. Pour the boiling syrup into the oven dish or divide equally amongst the four oven dishes.
7. Carefully spoon the batter into the hot syrup.
8. Bake the pudding for about 30 minutes for the large size, and 10 minutes for individual puddings, until golden.
9. Serve warm with cream or thin custard.

Chapter 11

P(M)Sish

This recipe makes the most gooey, decadent chocolate brownies imaginable. They give you such a chocolate fix that one of my students nicknamed them the PMS brownies. And the name stuck! And a word to the lads: if you have annoyed your missus, a tray of these will go a long way to patching things up. With chocolate as the mortar. The frozen raspberries work brilliantly as they stay whole during the baking process, adding bursts of pink tartness in the slab of chocolatey goodness.

P(M)S Dark Chocolate Raspberry Brownies

MAKES 1 TRAY

Ingredients:

- 150g butter, cubed
- 350g dark chocolate, broken into pieces
- 225g caster sugar
- 2 eggs
- 275g plain flour
- 1 t baking powder
- 1 T cocoa powder
- 250g frozen raspberries, don't defrost
- 1 T cocoa powder, for dusting

Method:

1. Preheat the oven to 160°C. Grease a deep baking tray with sunflower oil. Line with parchment paper, enough to hang over the sides. Oil the top of the paper too.
2. Melt the butter and 200g of the chocolate in a glass bowl over a pot of simmering water. Allow to cool slightly.
3. Sift together the flour, baking powder and cocoa powder.
4. Beat the eggs into the chocolate mixture then add the sifted flour.
5. Fold in the chocolate and raspberries.
6. Spread into the tin and bake for 30-35 minutes until just set.
7. Allow to cool before cutting into slices and dusting with cocoa powder.

Kitchen Kit

My kitchen at home is small with very little cupboard space, so I simply don't have room for useless electrical appliances and random kitchen gadgets. Of course, in my line, I still collect bits and bobs. But there are a few essentials that make preparing food easier and more pleasurable. When it comes to items like pots, pans and knives, it is very worthwhile investing in good brands. They will last many many years and give you loyal service. I mention brands that I use at home and in my cookery school.

Stainless Steel Pots

- 3 stainless steel pots :1 largeish one for pasta and soup, medium size , small

Non Sick Frying Pans

- A non stick chef's pan with a lid, this is rounded pan with a large capacity that can double up as a wok. I have a Circulon version that I've had for 10 years!
- A heavy based pan that's non stick inside and stainless steel outside so that it can go into the oven. I have a Stellar pan which is dishwasher safe too.
- A non stick crépe pan for omelettes and pancakes

Le Creuest Casserole Pots

- A`medium size casserole dish with a lid
- Individual baking dishes for individual pies etc
- A deep 'roasting' dish, round or rectangular

Bakeware

- Muffin tray
- Loose bottomed cake tin
- Loaf tin
- Baking Tray
- Losse bottomed pastry dish for tarts, quiches etc

Knives

- A chefs' knife, a filleting knife and a small serrated knife, kitchen scissors.
  I favour German brands like Henkel as the carbon content in the steel is very high, making them very hard wearing and resilient.
  Always wash your knives by hand as dishwashers make blades go blunt.

Tools
I favour OXO for the following (not the stock cube, but the kitchen brand!)

- Handheld mandolin
- Measuring jug
- Box grater
- Y shaped peeler
- Zester
- Salad spinner
- Apple corer
- Melon Baller

Microplane Grater
This is a highly specialised grater that will zest citrus fruit, grate ginger, garlic, lemongrass, Parmesan, nutmeg, chocolate and just about anything

Rubbermaid
Heat resistant silicone spatulas

Joseph and Joseph Garlic Press
the only garlic press I recommend

Odds and Ends

- Chopping boards
- Silicone baking sheet
- Potato ricer
- Citrus juicer
- Tongs
- Digital Weighing Scales
- Mixing bowls
- A small sauce whisk
- A balloon whisk
- Pin boning tweezers for fish
- Metal skewers
- A knife roll or magnetic strip for the wall to secure knives

Handheld Blender
or larger food processor like a Magimix
Handheld eggbeater
or larger mixer like a Kenwood

Preferred Suppliers

Glenisk Organic Dairy	www.glenisk.com
Top Fruit fruits and vegetables	www.topfruit.com
Miele Appliances	www.miele.ie
Arnott's Kitchenware and electrical goods	www.arnotts.ie
Jabula South African Shop and Online Store	www.jabula.ie
Biltong and Boerewors	www.biltong.ie
The Market Butcher	www.themarketbutcher.eu
Silverhill Duck	www.silverhillfoods.com
Kish Fish	www.kishfish.ie
OCHo Organic Herbs and Spices	www.organicherbco.com
Ballybrado Organic Oats and Spelt	www.ballybrado.com
Thai Gold Thai and Asian Products	www.thaifood.ie
Milleeven Honey	www.mileeven.com
The Hopsack Health Shop	www.hopsack.ie
The Organic Supermarket	www.organicsupermarket.ie

Weights and measurements

I only use metric measures, not pounds and ounces. But I do use several different methods for measuring. Normally liquids are measured by volume and you would use a measuring jug and measuring spoons. Solid ingredients are normally measured by weight, so you would use a weighing scales. But quite often, especially in old recipes, cup measures are used for both liquids and solids. As many of these recipes are family recipes, I have kept them in the format they were written. So here is a quick guide to the measurements.

T- tablespoon -15ml
t- teaspoon-5ml
1 cup-250ml
½ cup-125ml
¼ cup-75ml

You will need:

Measuring jug
Measuring spoons
Weighing scales, preferably digital

The recipes are written for convection, also known as fan ovens.